T0328494

as told to Amanda Ngudle

MAMKHIZE

MY WORLD MY RULES

African Perspectives Publishing
PO Box 95342, Grant Park 2051,
Johannesburg, South Africa
www.africanperspectives.co.za

© Shauwn Mkhize

ISBN PRINT: 978-1-998965-20-5
ISBN DIGITAL: 978-1-998965-21-2

Cover Image
Hair & Make Up: Melford Hlabola
Art Direction: Nikiwe Nyembe
Photographer: Philly Mohlala

Editors: Ree Ntuli
Karabo Kgoleng
Graphic Designer: Azile Maqwati
Typesetting: Phumzile Mondlani

CONTENTS

FOREWORD

No one can deny that South Africa has a deep, troubled and bloody past, a past that has left a deep scar on the nation's psyche that will yet take generations to heal. No part of this country went untouched; millions of the majority greatly suffered in the country of their birth merely because of the colour of their skin. The original inhabitants of this land were relegated to third-class citizens who had to walk around with a piece of paper to prove their meagre privileges, who were segregated by unjust laws and had to live in squalor; who had to be satisfied with the crumbs of education and healthcare; and who were thought only good enough for menial labour.

Yet, thankfully, many South Africans and their families played an integral role in this country's struggle for political freedom. The same is true for the subjects of this very compelling story who have a proud tradition of involvement in, and contribution to the struggle. The sons and daughters of the soil to whom we shall be eternally grateful.

Many individuals, families, political, civic and religious formations contributed to the struggle against apartheid - countless big and small contributions. So many of our people paid the ultimate price, and this family certainly paid a steep price; only more is the pity that this sacrifice is lost in the current day South Africa where the liberators of yesteryear are stealing from the poor masses.

Yet, good lives are lived. In and amongst the tears there is laughter and joy. Children are born into this world, families are built, and they grow, despite the hardship. This world, which we are fighting to make a better place; much as the people of this entire story have done and the author is attempting to do through her own life - tribulations and contributions.

It is marvellous that the author of this book has taken the brave step of writing her and her family's history. It certainly is an interesting read in a nice colloquially written style that is easily palatable. I applaud her for exposing the inner sanctum of her thoughts to a possibly critical public because it serves not only as a recording of historical facts from her perspective but also gives us an idea of the zeitgeist during apartheid from a child's perspective; the physical, mental and psychological effects of that monstrous system.

Yet, one might argue that her experiences, trials and tribulations have made her the woman she is today; one strong enough to bare her soul to us.

Bantu Holomisa
MP and President of the United Democratic Movement

May 2022

DEAR MAH

Dear Mama,

"It has taken me a long time to gather the words to pour into this letter, mah. I think about you every day, remembering your infectious laughter, your courageous spirit and your brilliant mind. You were so way ahead of your time, and on top of that, you loved us dearly. You were a proper hen. Given how full your days were, it is a wonder you were still able to shower us with so much love and attention.

I also think of the other side of you, the side of the lioness. There has never been a mother like you; one who could juggle a machinegun and a baby on her back. In my colliding memories, I sadly always recall that fateful night, the one that altered our lives forever. Was dad watching it all from above? Did he see his friend pleading with you and saying he would take us without you if you chose to stay behind? What about when you came running in your nightgown at the eleventh hour? You were a force yazi mah?

It is not my wish to worry you about what should have happened, but I wish I had asked and told you about these things in the aftermath. I should have told you it was not until morning that sleep finally came. I spent the entire night tossing and turning, in total disbelief of what had befallen us. How like a thief in the night, we had been robbed of our lives. At first in portions then last night, a total ambush. Why did you not call your comrades to come and protect us because the arson was a long time coming, mah? Did you not believe it would really happen and be so severe?

It was remarkable to see your strength through this ordeal, mah. I cannot imagine how high the tales were after our narrow escape. I know you didn't care for small-town talk but were you even aware of the relish of our lives by people looking from the outside? The questions were spectacular! Most of the things we were asked were so ridiculous we didn't bother relaying them to you anymore. I wish I had developed a one-way response and said, "Be careful of what you wish for". Don't get me wrong mah; you gave us a great life. Besides a few horrors, I would not trade my childhood for anyone else's. However, there were times when we were terrified. Like when we were attacked halfway

6

through eating a meal. I wonder how you kept your wits about you. Was it all part of an elaborate plan to keep us blissful in our childish ignorance?

I was thinking of the biblical story of Lot's wife that night, the way we were asked to sprint off without looking back only for our home to burn down to ashes a few hours later. Did you have any hope that we could salvage stuff from the ashes? I'm so glad I wasn't there when you went to see for yourself the utter destruction..."

People think I downplay my privilege when I tell them about my childhood. They think I should lay out the red carpet leading to an elegant entrance of our gracious farmhouse and take them along the fairy-tale. It was a mansion, yes, but we were not raised to mention our pleasures; that was tantamount to bragging about your partner's education according to my folks.

No amount of modesty could pacify the community of Umbumbulu though, a small town south of KwaZulu-Natal. Some people were seriously ticked off. The village was a favourite with potential farmers because of its fertile soil and sweetgrass for livestock. Political, ethnic and clan wars were sporadic and were defused as soon as they had ensued—but not before serious bloodshed and displacements. Nonetheless, the engine of life hummed on. We went to school and businesses continued to grind.

The newly built house stood majestically with big, airy rooms that soon started to accommodate strangers and family friends alike. Built for comfort and hospitality, it drew uncles and aunts we would later understand to be the political struggle comrades of our parents. Activists fleeing the apartheid security forces were often accommodated before moving along. The likes of Bheki Cele, Jeff Radebe, Zweli Mkhize and human rights lawyers such as Griffiths and Victoria Mxenge were amongst the hundreds of familiar faces who frequented our house. Some were either en route to exile or other political activities. Some had pending investigations or meetings with my parents. Our house was a beehive of activity.

Before becoming a political think tank venue and a weaponry bank, our house was just a normal beautiful home with six bedrooms, a kitchen, lounge and dining room upstairs for magnificent views. We had drivers, helpers and white gardeners and mechanics. We could have been the Carringtons or the Forresters; dynasty families from my childhood soapies, except ours was a true story. So true that our nanny, Fikisiwe had a very low tolerance for disobedience. My goodness, she scolded, punished and even gave us occasional hidings.

"Did you give her a specific instruction not to spare us the rod, mah? Because if you did, I'll have you know that she took full advantage of that authority. She was your ears, your eyes and your third hand. Others never touched us. Anyway, mah, I have to thank you for giving us such a dignified upbringing. Please tell dad that his business not only brought us wealth, but it also brought us unknown faces and made us subjects of astonishing curiosity from the locals. For children our age, this helped open our world even wider. We learnt early not to get too attached to people who came and went. The wool of ignorance about what was happening in the world around us was removed far too soon despite there being a deliberate but subtle mission to keep us out of the festering turmoil. There was still no stopping our young minds from noticing glaring facts..."

We observed from a young age that our mom was a political paragon of strength. Especially after the death of my dad who was brutally murdered by a well-known thug in a police uniform called Siphiwe Mvuyane. She was left to take care of four children and businesses all by herself before she was 40. While some people would have cowered and immersed themselves in the grief that typically envelopes widows, she went back to the drawing board and carried out dad's wishes: there would be a black president in this country and black people would be liberated from apartheid's rule of perpetual monstrosity.

Others remember family album photos with musky nostalgia. I look at the few salvaged photos from relatives and remember, with great sadness, how our children will never know our history and ancestors. Otherwise, my memory goes to the time we were rudely awoken and bundled to the floor together by big, tall white policemen demanding to be shown ammunition that was to be used for political retaliation. Other times, I picture them asking us to hand over "communists" at large. I sadly remember the use of violence towards us and my own parents' use of firearms to fight enemies firing from the shadows. It was like living in an action movie.

With every attempt on our lives, my bespectacled, tough-as-nails mom calmly held meetings with men in suits whose respect for her bordered on fear. In the eye of women's oppression, my mother spoke fearlessly and called out cowardice. The struggle continued. When dad was still alive, he would also confuse the enemy by continuing with his everyday life of running his trading store, sugarcane farming and taxi and bus businesses as if nothing had happened. He was a political smooth operator. And together they were unstoppable.

My paternal grandfather, Yeli Mkhize left his wife MaHlengwa with seven children. My dad was the fourth child. In another village, MaHlengwa would have been subjected to a culturally arranged marriage called ukungenwa; a custom that requires the widowed or abandoned wife to remarry into the same family, usually to the brother of the dead husband/deserter or the next available male relative in order to preserve marriage and lineage that already exists after a spousal's death. In the case of the widower, the sister to the late wife "takes over her sister's house" as the new wife.

This practice meant foregoing numerous traditional ceremonies typically held as a way to blend the new wife into her new family or worse, necessitate the change of identity documents, a mammoth task in the old regime. I have heard of people whose surnames were changed completely by the misspelling of their surnames. The ramifications went as far as having the family mistaken for an entirely different ethnic group. We never met our paternal grandparents, unfortunately. It was a wonder to many who saw dad's dazzling business acumen and deft fathering skills later in life. He never worked for another man a single day in his life and began his legacy by selling clothes that bore numerous other businesses later.

As a nurse, my mother had a remarkable dual personality. She was a caregiver at work and a fearless fighter out there. Affectionately known as 'Mam Flo' later in life, she was born in 1942 in Kwa-Hlabisa, North of Kwa-Zulu Natal. Her parents, Jotham and Andrina Manqele expected a boy when, to their surprise, my mom was born. So they gave her a fitting name, Dumazile (a disappointment). She, fortunately, had other names to go by; Grace and Florence. The first of five children, she trained as a nurse at the McCord Hospital after finishing her basic education. Then she met my clothing businessman dad in the late 60s and they married in 1969. They were 27 and 28 respectively. Later, my three siblings and I were born. I am the second last child. S'bu was born in 1970, Nozipho in 1973, I in 1975, and Sphelele in 1986.

United by love and an unwavering political spirit, the young and ambitious comrades initially settled in Lamontville township where they had a four-bedroom house and started raising their young family.

We heard that my mother led from the front, having been involved in the struggle against apartheid before most people had the foresight and willpower for politics. I heard that at only 20, mom became the Apartheid government's persona non grata for participating in the Defiance Movement after joining the Congress Movement.

I'm not sure when we moved to our farm in a village called Sobhisi, in Umbumbulu. Nevertheless, this is where we all remember our formative years. We had a great life. My mother's ideas were grand. They went beyond the parameters of her yard. I am particularly in awe that she even participated in the writing of The Freedom Charter. Her vision was not for the benefit of only those close to her. The liberation and empowerment of women were always high on my mom's agenda because her vision was bigger and of course mostly because her thinking was way ahead of her time. So, she worked underground with the likes of Helen Joseph and Dorothy Nyembe under the Federation of South African Women (FEDSAW). The other campaign that family members praised my mom's bravery so highly for was the Release Mandela Campaign in Natal, back in the 70s.

"Kids at school would run to us with a newspaper bearing a photo of you, mah and heighten my street cred but thankfully, I was too young to realise what all this activity entailed and the actual threat it posed on your life. I'm sure there were many relatives, friends and neighbours who feared that your fate was an early grave and that we would one day be raised without you. I thank the bliss of ignorance for this. Otherwise, I would have been a hindrance, crying on your heels and holding your dress by its hem. The papers said you were one of the founding members of the United Democratic Front (UDF) in 1983, a time when political turmoil was at an all-time high in this province. People all over South Africa lamented the horrific political disaster. The news on TV said Natal was at the forefront of the most violent and growing number of killings. They said it was not uncommon to hear of an overnight attack on an entire family, their crops and animals.

I know mental wellness was not your specialty, otherwise, I know you would have led a mental wellness campaign for the children of the struggle in the same way that Luciano Pavarotti raised awareness and funds for the children of Bosnia and Yugoslavia. Many people who were children at the time struggle to conjure up the right words to describe how they were affected by the violence between members of the Inkatha Freedom Party (IFP) and the African National Congress (ANC/UDF) alliance."

Even without bloodshed, which was mostly inevitable, lives were sadly interrupted when families had to move towns and start afresh in places that were remote and mostly underdeveloped. It was worse for kids who did not even know the entire story and the reasons for their uprooting which happened sometimes more than once and overnight. Others lament the number of funerals they endured. Some children were left to fend for themselves and didn't know where their next plate of food or meals would come from.

"Yes, some say they grew accustomed to the traumatic stories but like us, they were not allowed the opportunity to process the incidents so that they could pack that chapter of their lives away and brace themselves for the next. Trauma has continuous ramifications. For instance, I choose to deal with the trauma by shutting the bad memories away instead of going towards them and resolving their residue in my head. But I'm okay, mah. We are well and solid. Your love for us has kept us going..."

DEAR BABA

Dear Baba,

"You were gone too soon, dad. They say life begins at 40 and ironically, that's when yours was ended. I remember your ways like you never left. If I knew that the day at the Umbumbulu police station holding cells would be our last together, I would have at least taken a photo even though it would have burnt down with the house like the rest of our precious possessions. If money could buy a life, I would spend my life working day and night to make sure you stayed because I refuse to believe that your job was done on earth; you still had so much to offer.

Thank you for showing us we had as much right and chance at prosperity as everyone else; for not moulding us to think wealth belongs only to white people like most black people were conditioned to think back then. You do not understand how by just being a successful entrepreneur during those difficult years, when all the odds were stacked against black people, you automatically shared the Bluetooth of success and bravery with us. You made us believe that wealth was everyone's right. Simultaneously, these very virtues; your sophisticated ways of doing things and your success made you Umbumbulu's worst nightmare. Did you know this? Thinking back, I have no way of knowing for sure because you were always such a gentleman.

Did you realise, that even though it wasn't your intention, you made grown men feel small by building this six-bedroom castle we called home? This was apparent when your friends proudly called you Motoziyaduma from your prolific collection of cars. Where did you get such ambition and the courage to carry out your grand wishes when you were so young and faced with so much adversity? You and mah were the greatest. Please tell her I thank her for choosing you..."

Two clans actively wanted us banished from Umbumbulu because even though my dad hailed from Lamontville township, a mere 34 kilometres away, the locals still considered him as a foreigner. Over and above that, he was a youngster in his 30s. So deep and urgent was the hatred that we soon started dealing with gun attacks. We often had to take cover in the middle of studying and sometimes on a Sunday evening. Who plans to kill people on a Sunday? It took a strong character to live with us. Our nannies would sometimes leave as if to visit their families on a Friday, never to return.

We should have just sold the farm and left in the middle of the night but nope, my parents had other ideas. That kind of bravery is both a gift and a curse. It is the kind of gallantry that borders on insanity. It was as if you put the struggle first and as an afterthought, were grateful your family was still alive instead of the other way. My diehard parents must have thought of their rural attackers as small fry, so giving up was out of the question.

In the meantime, all security measures were put in place. We had to tread carefully as children. Although it wasn't directly communicated, we understood that we couldn't have other children play in our home. It's also a possibility that they were warned by their own families to not come too close to our family. We never walked to school. A designated driver was assigned the responsibility of transporting us to and from school. I heard many of our fellow pupils wished to be us because of our neat uniforms, mouth-watering lunchboxes and chauffeurs at our beck and call. Unbeknown to them, we wished for a normal life of just being kids. The freedom to walk with our backpacks on our backs, cracking jokes, making pacts and running this and that way. We longed to be normal children with little people problems instead of grown-up ones.

Worse were the school trips. We were those children with a car that drove behind the expedition bus and missed all the song, dance and mischief on the bus. Love letters never reached us, and everyone knows how boys like trying their luck when away from school. The Tiger Balm myth remained a fable. We grew up hearing that if a boy smeared a little of the balm on a girl's thigh, she would instantly fall in love and run after him. Self-made alcohol using Appletiser and Disprin were legends we never found proof of either.

War cries were things we learned upon arrival at any sports event. On rare occasions, we heard "Sizobabamba sibashuka-shuke sibalahlele phezulu!" and "Niyabesaba na? Hayi asibesabi siyabafuna!" all the way to the hosting school. All because our family was under siege. Why are so many hearts engulfed in hatred?

"To make up for lost childhood time, you took us to the beach where you gave us the best memories. In those days, I didn't see many present fathers, nor did I see many black people enjoy the beach. I realise now, that because you were your own boss, you had the freedom to allocate time to priorities as you pleased. Beach trips were precious, baba. It's so unfortunate that all the photos we took got lost in the fire. I know now that memories are priceless.

I always wondered if you liked your mother-in-law. Most fathers did not. It doesn't matter. Thanks for letting us connect with our maternal family in Kwa-Hlabisa. Here, we were allowed to be proper children. First came Granny Andrina's annual colon cleansing which consisted of detoxing with herbs, or a sunlight soap and water concoction given through the rectal end in a rubber syringe. It was embarrassing to us but what could we do? Mom was never one for these rituals, but in Gogo's homestead, she had no say, and she knew better than to overstep boundaries."

My granny would allow us to eat anything and roam free with other kids. There was a stream down the hill that produced the sweetest mangoes on its banks during the festive season. All the village children met there to help themselves to the gifts of nature. We would run and swim without a care in the world.

Gogo made it her duty to teach us about decorum. We laugh about that now. There was nothing she hated more than girl children who didn't know how to sit with their knees together. Sitting carelessly is referred to as "ukugovoza" in isiZulu, loosely translated to showing your weapons or swearing without saying a word.

Thankfully, that is where cultural imposition ended for us. In other villages in KwaZulu-Natal, girl children were subjected to the controversial ritual of "ukuhlolwa" a practice of virginity testing. Some would be forced to open their legs from as early as the age of five. I cannot think of a more humiliating experience. The initial intention was honourable and was based on the African archangel known as Nomkhubulwane. The nobility of the practice was to preserve girl children's purity. This in turn pleased the ancestors and Nomkhubulwane.

Boys, on the other hand, were circumcised as a mark of manhood, a coming of age. However, the practice soon came to a halt after the prevalence of wars during the reign of King Shaka. Conscription meant there was no room for abscondment, not even for medical reasons such as recuperating from circumcision. Thanks to democracy, today both boys and girls have some choice whether to follow these maturity milestone practices. Young men especially have the advantage of circumcision in the privacy and sterility of a hospital.

When the holidays were over, our cousins had gone back to their homes and we had come back from Kwa-Hlabisa, to kill boredom, we turned ourselves into a team of four musketeers and made do with each other's company. We played and were naughty together. We were happy. Especially when our house became an operational base for the comrades. Their comings kept the fires burning. Mom could be seen supervising a catering team of helpers and relatives and we knew we would eat like kings and queens later that day. Other times she rolled the dough and baked cakes herself and we would look forward to an early Christmas of VIP visitors.

Respect was paramount in our parents' upbringing of their children. We were already respectful children who pumped brakes at the approach of an adult and spoke to elders in the third person. We were particularly at our most impeccable behaviour when we had visitors. Mischief, burping, slouching, farting, gawking and feet dragging were not allowed. Even though my mother was a nurse with so much to do, she still kept a hawk's eye on us and ran a tight ship.

She still managed to farm furiously, producing sweet potatoes, mielies and amadumbe or taro roots, a local delicacy. She even had livestock that had designated staff to look after them. But she would still manage to get her hands dirty from taking care of the cattle, the sheep and the goats herself. I think the rural girl in her made her look at farming as the completion of her wifely duties or farming just ran through her veins. Hard work is said to be therapeutic for some people.

One of the things I hugely admired about my parents was their unwavering support in whatever we chose to do. Many people can be trained and workshopped for the jobs they find themselves in, but no employee delivers with more joy than one who does what they love for a living. Mom was a nurturer and dad did what he loved doing, making money and using it for the upliftment of others.

As a couple, my mom and dad were not sidetracked by their domestic duties; they were madly in love, but this isn't something you could capture with a camera. They were old school. I suspect touchy, feely moments were nocturnal activities. What was at the top of their agenda was a vision for a better country and a better life for all. To unpack their compatibility, you had to scrutinise what drove their choices and the people they fraternised with in business, careers and the things to which they dedicated their lives. These things must have drawn them together in the first place. I imagine that they shared all these values because home was blissful.

"In hindsight, I realise how mah and baba had no time to be like the couples we watched on television. You made us grasp the true meaning of a calling. You couldn't drop the ball because you had a social responsibility to balance the scales between the haves and the have-nots. I am grateful that you did not exhibit this generous spirit by just throwing money on church donations but by empowering those who could achieve these for the people en masse. Were you in love with the political struggle or did you figure there was no going back? Either way, I am in total awe of your gallantry. I would have loved to see mom and dad grow old together like other couples. My only prayer is that you are reunited in love and have the job of nothing else but to be with each other, have many tender moments and forget about the troubles of the world because you both ran a good race. We love you, Baba."

REALITY STRIKES

Every child believes in the hourglass predictability of sand that slides through the same pace and fashion day in, day out. Unless they are living in a time of a raging war or have lived through a dark trauma, they have no reason to believe that their lives will be disrupted, never to rehabilitate.

Having survived numerous attempts on our lives, I always thought the sun would rise in the east again and we would take our positions on the table before taking off to seize the day. As in my favourite soapie families, we could always conquer the storms. The sun would set in the west, ushering for us all our well-deserved peaceful rest as we retired to our beds in anticipation of the following day. But as they always say, the one thing you can be sure of in life is change. Something peculiar did happen and it changed our lives entirely and forever.

A series of incredible events went from lull and straight into the fast lane. Do you know that life event that pulls the carpet from under your feet? First, on a day that showed no signs it would end the way it did, my older brother S'bu fought with a guy named Dede Ndaba in Umlazi. According to the helper and handyman who were home at the time, S'bu came home with a friend and dug out guns and ammunition buried by the comrades. Off they went to finish what had been started. How that played out, we will never know.

When we returned from school the following day, we were shocked to be met by every military vessel and police vehicle you can think of. Our home resembled a military camp depot. They came well-informed about the whereabouts of arsenal and took Nozipho who was 17 at the time because neither my dad nor mom was home. I was 15. Nozipho was taken and interrogated to reveal my dad's whereabouts. When she couldn't disclose his whereabouts, she was tortured. Of course, she had no idea where my dad was. He could have been anywhere. Our father was a businessman with numerous enterprises. But they held on to her, tormenting her with electrical points on her arms. When asked about distant relatives, Nozipho could only think of our aunt in Port Shepstone, about 120km from home. The long distance was no bother for the policemen on a mission. They drove her there and of course, my dad wasn't found. So, the pointless scourge continued.

She told us she was blindfolded, kept in unknown police cells and was only released on the third evening at a bus station not too far from home. She said after a while, she lost track of time. Reporting her absence was pointless. How do you complain to a tyrant about his wayward son? We saw her in the shadows on the night of her return, hiding like a wounded deer in the yard. Upon realising it was us, she threw herself at mom and we all cried and embraced her, happy to be reunited. Broken as she was by the ordeal, she was happy to be home again. She had wounds on her arm as proof of what she went through.

Oblivious to the torture suffered by his daughter, dad was in hiding at a friend's house in a neighbouring township called KwaMakhutha. We visited him the following day and upon seeing my sister's wounds, dad broke down and cried. I had never seen my dad shed a tear before then. Luckily, she was not raped, although she did say there had been an idle enquiry from one of the policemen about whether she was on her period.

Sick of living like a coward and following a meeting with his lawyer, dad handed himself over to the authorities. I'm sure no one had reason to suspect anything untoward with this turn of events. Comrades were always being shipped in and out of police stations for "further questioning."

The next day after school, Nozipho and I were driven to visit him at the Umbumbulu police station. The perverted police went beyond the call of duty in assisting us to see him in the cells. I'm sure their behaviour would have turned his stomach, but there were more pressing matters, and we already knew the country wasn't going to be liberated by us picking fights with the police or acting like damsels in distress.

Seeing our furrowed eyebrows, I remember how his first concern was for our wellbeing. He then expressed an ill feeling. Something about him being numb. As if on second thought, he said he was cold. He reassured us he would be okay and would return home to us soon. I was happy when he requested that we bring him a blanket after having spent the night in a freezing cell. It meant we would see him twice in the same afternoon. On our way home, we spoke about the injustice of an innocent person with a warm bed waiting for him at home spending a cold winter's night in a holding cell. He had done nothing to deserve any of this. We had no idea that things were about to get real.

Upon our return to the police station, we discovered that, like a bag of beans, our dad had been swiftly moved by one notorious trigger-happy, constable Siphiwe Mvuyane. By day, Mvuyane worked for the KwaZulu Police (KZP) and was stationed at the GG police station in Umlazi. By night, he carried out the most heinous crimes against ANC and UDF activists, with the support of KZP. His jurisdiction was endless. The mere mention of his name dampened the mood wherever you were. Talking about him meant people were reeling or fearing the worst in his wake.

The lawyer's car made a stop in our driveway four days later. We assumed it was to give us an update on where my dad had been moved to, how he was doing and what the legal team's next step would be. It turned out she had come to announce my father's death. It was surreal. Especially what followed. Mom was done for. She sobbed bitterly, all hope drained from her. I will never forget the horror. And then the lawyer left. The sun set.

After the distressing bawl, my mom gathered herself together and proceeded with the funeral arrangements. Some relatives were not keen to avail themselves; they feared for their own lives by association. She understood. That was the life of a political activist. This is why they associated themselves with comrades because only other comrades could be trusted at such times.

My dad's body was found on the banks of a stream in Umlazi township. He had been pumped with a bullet to his head. His hands were cuffed before his life was snuffed out of him. The day was June 12, 1991, and he was only 40, leaving behind a young widow to take care of four children. Or so we thought. It later emerged that he had fathered three other children.

Every violent death is devastating, but there is something particularly evil about killing a man without giving him a chance to fight for his life. Not that Mvuyane or any other bloodthirsty killer wants to give anyone a dignified death, but to the family of the deceased, it is both malevolent and cowardly.

I think it was on the same night that we heard the police station had been burnt down. Other reports said it was several police stations. According to the police, the main suspect was my brother S'bu for all of them. He fled the area immediately. So as the funeral arrangements were underway and relatives started pouring in, there was this mounting concern for S'bu's whereabouts and safety.

Everyone was overcome with grief. Needy locals were shattered because my dad was so benevolent he would often run at a loss from giving credit. He lent people money. I think it was his clothing and sugarcane businesses that sustained his trading store. He had also started trading in luxury cars, which he bought from auctions.

So torn were people by my dad's sudden death that they started likening it to that of a plot by a popular television drama of the time called Hlala Kwabafileyo. Like the main character, shop owner Zakhe Mhlongo, they hoped and peddled a desperate rumour that his death had been a bizarre case of mistaken identity. Black people have never been good at taking sad news in their stride, especially death announcements. There was a bereavement programme on the radio that was presented with such gloom and sadness you couldn't help but ponder on the ever-presence of death in life for days on end. Hearing the programme that week, cut deeper.

I must say the resemblance of the Mhlongos' to our story was uncanny. Even Mhlongo's wife was MaMkhize. Neighbours comforted us by reassuring us that dad would be found and come back to continue his remaining living days with his family and community. How we would have loved that ourselves! How nice it would have been to turn that television drama into reality! Instead, reality mounted with every step towards the day of the funeral, especially when the grave was dug and there waited a gaping hole to swallow dad's body.

S'bu made a secret appearance. The police caught wind of the news and soon flooded our yard with their cars again. We spotted them from miles away and hid him in the ceiling. They turned the place upside down. I'm sure they would have asked my mom to stand up from the mattress if it had occurred to one of them. The visit prompted S'bu to make a clean getaway again.

The day of the funeral was a revelation. The proceedings took place in a local hall, which felt like a classroom given the number of people who came to pay their last respects. There were cars, busses, minibuses and cross-border envoys with foreign numberplates. Diplomats, some of whom didn't even speak English also attended the funeral. The police were also out in numbers and stood at a distance while Umkhonto We Sizwe comrades, armed to the teeth, sang songs of freedom and resistance. We were hearing this from loudspeakers as we waited for the body at home. Before we knew it, there were gunshots. Sobhisi had become a warzone of guns fired from different sides and this continued for the entire day. It was so unnerving we thought it would never end. The funeral programme started at eight in the morning and dad was only buried at seven that evening. We buried him in the yard. I never seemed able to take my eye off that tomb; that heap of soil that had him hidden six feet under.

S'bu, who watched his father's funeral from a distance, heard he was a wanted man and that his head now had a price tag to it. This time, he didn't run. Instead, he armed himself and waited. As expected, they came looking for him. Instead of hiding behind his mom's skirt, he ran to the bush to find himself a perfect spot to strike back. He looked every bit like a soldier that day. I think he decided to go down fighting than live in fear for the rest of his life.

With our cousin Msizi Mkhize by his side, they fought against policemen who looked like they were recruited from every police station in the province. Really, I had never seen so many police uniforms. It was the police, their dogs and a helicopter. We watched all this from our yard as it happened on a neighbouring hill, which quickly became a battlefield. We were watching as a way of witnessing how our brother would lose his life in that historic moment. Gunfire exchange went on and on with every policeman's gun shooting and chasing after my brother.

Msizi went down after a while and S'bu perched himself on a rock and continued fighting. There was one bloodthirsty policeman who led the army and thought he could catch my brother alive. S'bu later narrated that he feared their aim was not to kill him but to capture and torture him until death. So he simply shot him in the forehead, sending his skull up in the air. What a horrific thing to see! His dog was next. The shock of the policeman's death sent his followers off in droves.

By now, the helicopter was above him with its occupants shooting at him, no longer interested in his live capture. He said he took out an AK47 which had stopped working earlier and shot at the helicopter twice, which we saw burst into flames and rip into two. Our hands moved from holding our faces to our heads in disbelief and horror. It's anyone's guess how many policemen died that day. From the number of helicopters that soon joined the scene; we knew he was still alive. Gun smoke obscured our vision. He said he escaped the bush on his stomach and simply walked towards a bakery truck where he hid between the crates of bread, leaving behind chaos and ammunition waste. He got off a few stops later after the truck escaped a roadblock. With the driver and his assistant oblivious to his presence, he said he simply walked into the cane fields before crossing a raging Umzimkhulu river and made it to Transkei, now known as the Eastern Cape.

THE FLIPSIDE OF LIFE

Our father had not even turned cold in his tomb when his dear friend, bab'Eden Mngadi rushed over with a stern warning for us to vacate the homestead as there was talk of torching it by members of the Inkatha Freedom Party (IFP). Our community knew that the IFP did not throw about idle threats. This was serious business and a matter of life and death. His own home was on the list of houses to be burnt that night as well.

My mother, being her strong self, felt she couldn't escape in the middle of the night like a chicken. This debate continued for a long while. She was in mourning and maybe still confused by the anguish. I suspect she was hoping she was in a bad dream. Since S'bu was missing, she had probably hoped for a sudden clandestine visit from him. Knowing her, it's possible that she was contemplating dying in her house with her boots on. I could picture her taking as much ammunition to open fire in retaliation.

In the end, Bab 'Mngadi said he was taking us to a place of safety with or without her. That is when she eventually gave in and joined us in the car in her nightgown. Her love for us won in the end and out into the night we finally plunged. Thankfully, in my late dad's Mercedes Benz and not on foot as it happened to so many. With our school bags and a few clothing items on our backs, we drifted into the belly of the night wondering what tomorrow held in its hand of many mysteries.

That's why I didn't sleep a wink that night. I wondered if we still had a home to go back to. I couldn't stop thinking about my mom's dejection as she relented. There's nothing worse than seeing a hero on her knees. Was it fair that she had forfeited a normal family life and fought for every black man's justice only for her to have to pay so dearly in the end? We were in the throes of twilight.

We moved to Mbokodo's house. He was a white mechanic who fixed and maintained my dad's ploughing tractors. No one would guess our new location. We heard our house was up in flames roughly three hours after we left. All our belongings, our safety and some of our memories were burnt down to ashes as happened to so many other households. The cars, the trading store, the taxis, the buses and the sugar cane fields were also burnt down. We were distraught.

It was not long before our new location was said to be leaked and we swiftly moved into an orphanage in Sydenham. Bab'Mngadi and the rest of his family were there too, having lost their belongings in a fire for having housed my dad when he was a fugitive. We stayed there, living a new and empty life for approximately three months before we were moved to another orphanage in Verulam.

By now, Nozipho had gone to study at the University of Transkei. We heard that S'bu had also enrolled for a law degree but was now going by another name. The twilight continued. There was also a time when we lived in a room in Lamontville. Imagine living in one single room with everyone and that room serves as the bathroom, the kitchen, the lounge and the bedroom for all three occupants.

All this sojourning happened while my mom was adhering to all the rules and regulations imposed on African widows. Our culture is strict about what can and cannot be done in mourning regalia. Some rules have been eased over the years. Even the duration is no longer a full year. Back in the day, widows had to live like convicted witches during the duration of their mourning.

Regulations of mourning required widows to:

Wear black clothes from top to bottom for a year

Shave their hair

Give way when meeting others on pathways

Avoid people's homes

Lower their voices and gaze when talking to others

Avoid the front seats of private or public transport

Stay away from the livestock kraals

Take the very last pew at church and not stand about to greet others dressed like that

Stay away from the crops

Not carry newborn babies in their arms

Not leave their homes to spare others the bad omen and many more.

Widows mourning were believed to carry bad luck until a cleansing ritual was performed for them. So deep and widespread was this belief that chiefs could cut their mourning period to even a month if the mourning period started towards the spring season fearing that bad luck could prevent the first rains and cause a drought. The suffering was not reserved for African widows.

To this day, some Portuguese natives require a widow to wear black for the rest of their life. In some Nigerian tribes, the widow is made to drink the corpse's bathing water to prove her innocence in his death. If she dies from it, she's guilty and she if lives, well she has something to remember him by for the rest of her life now, doesn't she? It gets worse for others. In ancient Hinduism, a tradition called Sati required widows to be thrown in their husband's pyre to be burnt with them. This tradition started with a willing Sati who couldn't bear the death of her husband Lord Shiva and as a protestation towards her father's detestation for him. It later became a forced practice for widows. Those who died without children who could take care of them later in their twilight years were particular targets.

Meanwhile, universally a widower is free to roam the streets within weeks of his wife's passing. In fact, widowers are encouraged to do so to improve their chances of finding another wife and pick up where their life left off. This patriarchal practice remains uncontested because once your husband dies; you receive zero ears or sympathy from society. If anything, most women become first suspects for the death of their husbands. Take the issue of the late Bruce Lee's death. The first suspect for his untimely death was a woman known as Betty Ting-Pei, a fellow actress who was his girlfriend at the time. Investigations later revealed that Raymond Chow who had prior financial squabbles with Bruce had been on his premises at the time of his death. No one was found guilty.

We were having our own share of unbearable pain. There were no more nannies and drivers around us. We grew up overnight because mom was now all by herself and we had to pull our weight and do the things she couldn't and be where she wasn't allowed to be. We managed to chip in, but we were still down and withdrawn and therefore couldn't mix with other children. Through the window, I would watch other kids play down the road. The weather would be perfect for introducing myself, but I was just too terrified of the new environment. The very idea of starting over left me weak and utterly paralysed. A part of me felt that change was inevitable, but I had no idea about the first thing to do in this new chapter.

We were so emotionally incapacitated that even going to the shops was a mission. I held on to Nozipho's skirt when she visited as she herself moved in haste and stumbled. When I remember those little girls inside us, I feel like hugging them. I don't wish that era of our lives on my worst enemy.

On top of everything else, there was this dark cloud hanging over us. S'bu kept coming in and out of the province. We knew the police who were looking for him wanted him dead or alive. This meant that he was a dead man walking. His photo was in the newspapers, and he sometimes made headline news on the radio. I wonder how many people were tortured for his whereabouts.

There is a Zulu saying that is often directed at women, as they get ready for their marriage, and it says, "Umfazi uyibamb'ishisa!" Loosely translated, it means no matter how hot the pot in her hands is a woman doesn't drop it. My mom was the ambassador of that domestic law. There was no time for crying over her son or former home or the safety of her daughter at varsity. Nozipho was in great danger, especially when Mvuyane caught wind of her whereabouts and came to hunt her down. She told us the varsity authorities moved her to a third-year student residency.

My brother was living with a woman who treated him like her own son despite his unpredictable life. According to Nozipho, he attended classes but was not doing well because of his high level of distress.

One day not too long before, we had been a family of six in a lovely house with collector's cars in the garage and driveway. We had tea in golden China teacups upstairs, but here we were, a shrunken family of three without certainty there was still much to live for.

A different mother would have preferred exile to this bleakness. The circumstances we now lived under were usually the number one reason most comrades skipped the country. I'm sure mom had all the connections to take this option and I'm also certain her reputation would have guaranteed her a good spot in exile-friendly countries like Zambia and Angola, but she chose to stay and fight. With us under her wing, her determination could not be dissuaded.

Meanwhile, enlisted young white men called for military service wouldn't think twice about killing a fatherless family like ours. Funded by whites under the coffers called the security tax, they guarded the borders with the most dangerous arms you could ever think of. Their favourite method of killing was through bombs, which have tragically maimed members of Umkhonto We Sizwe trying to make it to the other side of the borders. Those who made it received better education, employment and political rank. But I suppose my mother had been so shaken by the tales, she chose to die in the country of her skull.

And so, we moved to yet another house before ultimately moving into a house my mother bought in Chatsworth. We had been fortunate enough that she had taken a house and contents insurance before our house was burnt down. From the payout, she was able to buy another house. We finally had a place to call home after such a long time of living in so many different places.

BILLY THE KID

Christians always preach that God will never give you a burden bigger than your ability to carry it. However, when people commit suicide, is it not proof that we are not always equipped to deal with some circumstances? My brother S'bu, who was only 20 at the time, had lost it and went on a witch-hunt for Mvuyane after my dad's body was found. After burning down the police stations, he made a clean getaway and sent a very clear message that he would never hand himself over, no matter how much immunity he was guaranteed. He abhorred the arrangement after our father ended up with a bullet in his head, following advice for him to hand himself over.

This was at the time when Mvuyane's killing spree had reached its height. Moreover, his murders were not limited to the people in the province. People were now mentioning his name in places as far away as Eastern Transvaal, now known as Mpumalanga, and even Mozambique. Even the late radio veteran Bob Mabena is said to have had a rough brush with this man during one of his gigs as a deejay at a concert in Durban. Mvuyane apparently slapped him across the face for "hoarding" the attention of female concert revellers. He believed with everything in him that he owned the KZN social scene and its young women, mostly students. Mvuyane attended higher education parties and pageants as a man whose enemies hid in the night. Beautiful strangers were simply caught in the crossfire. If a beautiful girl caught his eye before he spotted his target, he had no problem hitting two birds with one stone. Meaning that he would catch his prey for the kill and still manage to help himself to the girl.

This legacy was not enough of a deterrent to S'bu's mission. In his quest to get to him, he single-handedly felled a few of Mvuyane's associates, colleagues and guerillas. He apparently used hand grenades and a firearm in his pursuit of vengeance. It was like a movie for the media. They called him "Billy the Kid" after the legendary movie character. In the true spirit of his movie character, S'bu seemed to have acquired a different mindset as he managed to evade the long arm of the law for almost a year, leaving havoc and mayhem in his wake. In a statement on the killing of dog unit warrant officer Peter Knop, S'bu sent investigators in all directions by planting false leads. On one such mission, he apparently called a police unit and pretended to be a deep throat giving them Billy the Kid's location somewhere in Lamontville. Spurred on by their own bloodthirsty ambition, the unsuitable unit of three policemen responded to the call and walked straight into a trap. Two were killed and one escaped by playing dead in a rubbish bin the entire night.

His actions did not go unnoticed. General Bantu Holomisa, who was the military head of state for the former Transkei at the time, organised to keep him in an undisclosed location and gave him a pseudonym. This is when he registered for a law degree. It proved to be a futile mission. He wasn't submitting assignments or sitting for exams because of his mission.

I am not sure what the long-term plan was. Perhaps there was hope that extenuating factors and his state of mind would earn him some form of leniency in the inevitable trial. Maybe they were buying him time. The country was charting towards a new dispensation so perhaps there was hope that under the new government, his case would receive the special care it deserved. Yet somehow, S'bu found out we were attending an evening event and perhaps he thought his target would also be there. I know he would want to protect us from Mvuyane at all costs. He must have had this dual mission when he crossed the Umzimkhulu River that day. For homelands that had a border gate, S'bu's movements were ridiculously easy. So, he made his way back and continued wiping out whoever stood in his way.

Before our father's death, S'bu was just a lanky happy-go-lucky boy who liked nothing more than dancing. He didn't just like it; he was very good at it and could have had a career as a choreographer. And because he was something of a lady's man, he was suave and stylish in his lean body. He would almost drown the entire house with Jazz cologne after taking a shower. I can almost see mom winking at the helper behind his back at this—that parental knowing mirth! There couldn't have been a more suitable mother for him too. Mom and S'bu shared a birthday, and my dad's birthday was only a day later on November 5.

However, there was more to him than appearances. He could have made a great legal eagle too, given his analytical mind and winning attitude. An excellent listener, S'bu never argued before getting all his facts right. Astrology says people born on the 4th of November are intelligent and perceptive. They look for career choices that showcase their ability with words and outgoing personality.

I hoped to God that he was practising his favourite words he preached, "Do not trust too much and be gullible." This he said with all the truths revealed to us, following the killing of our cousin Sthembiso Mkhize by my dad's former friend and now detractor who led enemies to our home to burn it down. The man hanged Sthembiso's head on a pole for all to see. Such savagery was madness. So, when S'bu avenged that killing he did so in the presence of the man's brethren - killing him in point-blank style - thereafter, simply walking off.

Before mom bought her house, there was a time when we lived in Verulam and S'bu came to see us. Nozipho had visited for the holidays. Our cousin and my brother's close ally, Bridgeman was also around. They now lived together in Transkei because, by association, Bridgeman was on the police's hit list too. We were so excited to see them that we all hopped into the car after my mother sent them for groceries in the neighbourhood shops. Ever her intuitive self, my mom warned against all of us being in one car. "What if the enemy sees this and decides to kill one of you?" she pointed out. "Have you not heard of stories of a group of people all dying in an accident when the target was just one person?"

My sister and I reluctantly got out of the car and allowed them to leave without us. Mom always expected the worst and true to her fears, S'bu came back in a police car. Bridgeman had been killed. Someone, most probably an undercover policeman, had made him hold a hand grenade. How? No one knows, but S'bu was in one of the supermarket aisles and just saw the thing in his cousin's hands explode and ran for dear life. The Mchunu family – who were locals – gathered the body and took it to the mortuary because my family collecting it would have meant the end of us. This is when we moved to Lamontville overnight.

Naturally, S'bu had to disappear again. Before crossing the border into Transkei, he had an errand to run. In a moment of chance, he walked straight into a trap. Those who have been in the struggle often talked about how the blood on the streets presented an opportunity to make money. Capitalists often find loopholes and use the vulnerability of people to their advantage.

It turns out that he forgot to live by his word of not letting his guard down when he, together with our cousins, Sandile Mkhize and Nyamazane Njoko made a stop at an Indian runner's house in Isipingo for some money. The runner had been assigned to collect the taxi rank rental fees and peace committee's funds. My dad had built a taxi rank in Isipingo and also established the committee after restoring peace between warring taxi organisations and through delegates, managed the running of both enterprises. Of course, the man had helped himself to the funds upon my father's death and he must have seen S'bu as a threat when he stopped over that day for the collection. It didn't hurt that he would be paid handsomely for handing my brother over, so how could he refuse? Plus, the reward for his head had multiplied over time. It is believed that the runner secretly made the call to the police from his landline before S'bu's and our cousins' arrival.

We heard on the radio and from eyewitnesses that the scene at the runner's house turned into a war zone in no time. According to reports both official and unofficial, there were numerous vans, military tanks, a dog unit, a bomb squad and even a helicopter before an epic gunfire exchange ensued. I read numerous media reports alleging that S'bu was a hoodlum who died in an exchange of gunfire in a car chase. Some argue that he died in a hail of bullets in a house he was "holed up in". Others say he was killed when one of the tanks destroyed the house. The established fact is that S'bu, whose life had chosen him, gave the police warfare of a lifetime. The runner's neighbours said the young man gave them hell for hours before our cousins died and one bullet was heard to end it all.

My mom, a qualified nurse who went to view his body, confirmed that, from the positioning of his limbs, he had shot himself in the head. This is after he apparently ran out of the ammunition he carried with him in a backpack since the beginning of his being on the run. True to his promise, no one killed him, and he didn't hand himself over. He died with his boots on only after he had run a good race. It was July 1992, and he was 20 years old. He left behind four children, having lived way ahead of his time all his life.

The family asked Nozipho to come home and she heard about this epic warfare on the bus. My poor sister had to swallow it all and lock it inside throughout her trip. S'bu's funeral almost caused a stampede. People young and old, rich and poor, came to pay their last respects to S'bu Mkhize, not the son of a political activist, but a hero in his own right. We were growing accustomed to these big funerals. We were just not becoming accustomed to the extreme level of anguish each funeral ignited.

Meanwhile, Mvuyane's murderous journey would continue unabated. People mentioned is name during the most unpalatable conversations. Full-grown men sighed with relief when his car passed their homes with no harm done to them or their families. Whether he was from another killing or en route was a topic they would discuss later. For the moment, they held their breaths and hoped that their names were not on his hit list.

Female students in institutions of higher learning discussed that they were considering their options outside the KZN province because of stories of how he could just kidnap any girl, and nothing would be done about it. Wiser girls knew to co-operate to save their lives. Attempts at his life were futile. So much so, that there were talks that a firearm could not kill him. Some suspected that he used umuthi to immunise himself from bullet shots. How ironic is it that he was afraid of the very pain he inflicted so easily on others? This is very typical of cold-hearted killers.

Mvuyane wasn't the first to have reputedly used magic to avoid death by bullets. Former president of South Africa, Hendrik Verwoerd, one of the notorious architects of apartheid who showed little respect for black people, was eventually killed by stabbing at the hands of Greek-Mozambican Dimitri Tsafendas. This after he had been widely rumoured to have employed the gun ammunition rituals of the famous inyanga known as Khotso Sethuntsa from Lusikisiki, Transkei. The rumour started after many alleged attempts at his life, one well known having been the daring broad daylight shooting by businessman, David Pratt. Two closely charged bullets inexplicably went through his cheek and ear, leaving his enemies confused and more determined.

Where and how Mvuyane received his traditional shield was not known. How this manifested in his arrogance was something to behold. He even bragged in a newspaper interview that his body count was well above twenty but less than fifty. That is not to say he didn't maim others and leave them for dead.

During the Truth and Reconciliation Committee (TRC), one of his victims gave testimony of how Mvuyane shot him in the knee and forced him to stab himself repeatedly before shooting him in the arm where he bled copiously before leaving him for dead. There was also an incident in which he shot a high school pupil named Austin Zwane, execution-style and in front of his parents. The age and gender of his victims were never a bother to him.

There is no denying that trauma propelled my brother's actions. We all have different thresholds for suffering. S'bu's trauma manifested itself in irrational revenge. "I'm not black, I'm not white, not foreign, just different in the mind. Different brains, that's all," says the movie character, Billy the Kid and indeed just like him, S'bu acquired a different mind after my dad's death.

It is not clear how Mvuyane met his fate that early morning of May 1993. Apparently, he was enjoying his favourite pastime, attending an outdoor concert at the Durban Westville parking lot when he started complaining of dizziness and fatigue. Strangely, he refused his goons to accompany him that morning as he made his way to the car to "take a nap". They also strangely allowed a visibly sick man to be on his own. A few minutes later, gunshots sounded, and his friends found him oozing blood from a bullet wound to the head. He died on his way to the hospital. Whether he killed himself or someone else pulled the trigger remains unconfirmed. I only know that it was the end of a reign of terror for many families.

ALL ADO ABOUT NOTHING

Three years later, the Truth and Reconciliation Committee (TRC) was formed. One of its key pillars was to investigate human rights abuses between 1960 and 1994 and to apply for criminal and civil amnesty through the Amnesty Committee. Former president of the country, P.W Botha called it a circus and shunned any attempts to make him appear before the commission. His defiance resulted in a mere fine and a suspended sentence that was overturned on appeal. He remained free despite having reigned during one of the most oppressive and bloodiest eras. The TRC granted amnesty to people who had committed heinous, unprovoked crimes; people who killed for money and people who helped carry out killings of children and women. All while my brother lay stone cold in a tomb somewhere in Lamontville.

You ask yourself a lot of questions. Why was violence so necessary? How did people like Botha escape prison when they orchestrated so many killings? Our country has all the makings of a disaster because very few people, if any, have healed from the rule of apartheid. It is easy to say that apartheid did not make people fight. Yes, it did. It also planted weapons in the hands of people who had no clue about where the country came from or where it was going.

Ours was not a unique case of anguish. So many families gave chilling testimonies about the killing of their children right before their eyes. Others died on their way to exile because askaris had sold them out while some lost limbs and bodily functions due to letter bombs. During this entire process, many hoped the conclusion would involve some form of compensation or recourse from perpetrators but all they received were empty apologies.

The Mxenge couple, lawyers who spent their short lives defending the rights of oppressed South Africans to exist in conditions of freedom, justice, peace and democracy, died at the hands of death squads. As husband and wife, they lived their lives defending ANC members in different cases. They fought for justice for those at the forefront of the struggle. The notorious Vlakplaas base commander Dirk Coetzee ordered a killer squad to murder them in the most brutal fashion. Griffiths Mxenge died in 1981. He was abducted before apartheid assailants stabbed him 45 times, beat him with a hammer and slit his throat. His body was discovered near a soccer field in Umlazi.

A few months later, his wife, Nonyamezelo Victoria Mxenge, who jilted her nursing career in favour of a career in human rights law, was hacked right in front of her two small children in their Umlazi driveway. Four white men believed to be policemen, bearing axes, a bush knife and a gun left nothing to chance and took the job upon themselves.

A Durban magistrate refused to dignify her death with a formal inquest into her killing and ruled that she died of head injuries at the hands of "unknown persons". Ironically, the world would know of that murder through Mbongeni Ngema's stage production Sarafina! In the play, a teacher asks her students what they would like to present at the annual end-of-school-year event. They decide on a musical production, which would end with a song about Nelson Mandela coming home from prison and meeting the people on the Day of Liberation. They all want to play Mandela, but in the end, Sarafina regales her fellow pupils about her childhood idol, Victoria Mxenge, a black human rights lawyer, activist and widow. Sarafina tells how Mxenge won a court case for a black woman who had been raped by a white man by pointing out the prohibition of sex between blacks and whites. South Africa's Immorality Act came in handy and Mxenge cleverly won the case, which otherwise might have allowed the rapist to walk free. Sarafina acts out the rape scene as the other students echo the voice of the white man who scornfully demands of the black woman, "Why do you turn me down, girl when you are so emaciated that you're not worth looking at?"

Remembering Mxenge's brutal death, Sarafina screams out in horror, "Mama, Mama, Mama..." The others try to console her, and a melancholic song ensues. It is a harrowing scene—one that stays with you for long. This is how Mxenge's brutal murder and inevitably, her life and noble deeds are immortalised and are remembered the world over.

After exposing the existence of the unit, Coetzee went on the run, staying in 38 houses in four countries including a short stint in London where he joined the ANC. Coetzee was granted amnesty by the TRC and lived to be 67, having worked for a company called Edu Solutions supplying stationery to the Limpopo province. He died from liver failure and cancer.

Cardiologist Dr Wouter Basson dubbed Doctor Death headed a deadly campaign named Project Coast aimed at black people. He worked under P.W. Botha who hired him to head a specialist division of the South African Military

Services with primary targets being the South West Africa People's Organisation (SWAPO) prisoners through deadly chemical concoctions. As many as 200 people died from these particular attacks. In the 1980s, Basson and his thugs were allegedly involved in attacks and assassinations against incalculable members of anti-apartheid organisations. Leaders in South Africa, Angola and Namibia claimed that Project Coast used the more dangerous chemicals for what was referred to as "crowd control" in the country.

Not only is Basson alive with no one targeting him with a price on his head despite the plethora of crimes committed, but also in January 2021, it emerged that he was gainfully employed by Mediclinic International. The private healthcare company was founded in 1983 in Stellenbosch. The TRC granted him amnesty for full declaration of his participation and testifying, testified against the apartheid government.

Ours and so many other aggrieved families, is to make sense of the life ahead of us and carry on. This is where questions of fate and faith come into play; heroes and victims as well as the shaky ground on which aggrieved family members are left to tread, prevail. Like other families who were dealt the heavy hand of multiple griefs, we allowed the currents of the raging waters of anguish pull us and cause us to tumble before throwing us onto the riverbanks of healing. With one foot in front of the other, we walked towards recovery.

It was good to hear that, after 27 years, National Prosecutions Authority (NPA) launched new investigations on TRC cases that are still pending. Justice and Correctional Services Minister Ronald Lamola said the Hawks appointed 34 investigators, and the NPA obtained special approval for 23 prosecutors to deal with these matters because some families are still bleeding.

As an adult, as a way of "ukugxwala emswaneni" a Zulu term meaning to bawl at the remains, I would visit my dad's grave in the homestead we deserted. We are people who talk to our ancestors about our victories and ask for forgiveness. We stay in communion with our dearly departed. We visit the graves for different purposes. Others will go and report their plans and ask for blessings. Every time I visited my father's grave, something curious happened. I would find a snake perched on his grave, which would naturally send me flying. I have not met a black person who is not petrified of snakes. This happened a few times and it would leave me so forlorn. When my attempts were aborted because of this awful snake, I sought counsel and discovered it was a sign; that I had to rebuild the homestead. In most cultures, the belief is that a snake or serpent, despite the way it is depicted in the Bible, has come to symbolise rebirth and eternity, especially in the dwellings of the departed.

Of course, the most natural thing for me was to start by exhuming my late brother's body and bring it for burial next to our father. Let me tell you something; this is not as easy a process as they make it look on TV. First, there is the emotional heaviness. Memories of this person when he was alive will haunt you to no end. Then comes the administration; the paperwork and the traditional protocols to that everyone must observe.

The red tape that comes with exhumation is most probably the reason why some families never received the bodies of family members who died in exile. First, you send an application to the Provincial Government in conjunction with the Metropolitan Council. Through a court order, which is not instant, a court may authorise the process after a waiting period of seven days. Meanwhile, you are expected to have obtained the necessary authorisation from the respective authorities. This period is also necessary to give the South African Police Services (SAPS) time to arrange for a police officer to be present at the time of the exhumation because you may not do so in the absence of a law officer. Remember to also hire people who know what they are doing as you can't just rip open a tomb and find that your pick eventually goes into the coffin. Sand can rot coffin wood in a matter of months. The experience would be too awful, adding trauma to an already difficult situation. It is also not a free procedure; you have to pay the state for the trouble. The good thing is, you can keep the grave for later use or, believe it or not - sell it.

Once the protocols were observed and a new burial took place with the necessary traditional rituals observed for my deceased brother, the snake never returned. Another beautiful end to an era of terror.

MY NAME IS SHAUWN

I was born on a Sunday, April 6, 1975. I read somewhere that parents of Aries children such as myself should be prepared to walk on the wild side. We don't do half-baked stuff. From a young age, we are independent thinkers, ungovernable even. Not out of disrespect but out of challenging the status quo. I wouldn't take it as far as challenging parents about why they did things in the manner they did.

My dizzy bravery could easily border on endangering myself. This always prompted unsolicited advice from S'bu who would say, "Don't trust too much and be gullible." He must have established this from the comrades who crammed our home and had experiences of some who turned out to be askaris or crossed political floors without warning. Nonetheless, there was nothing to worry about. People worried too much. You laughed out loud, they peered, you broke something, and they came closer. Adults and their supervision inclinations.

I was always swimming against the tide and people could usually find me in the corner of the underdog with the resolve to balance the playing field. I was the first to notice a hungry or sick child. I was that girl who would insist we should help. I was well dressed for my personality too. As a tomboy in pants and t-shirts, I could climb trees, run for miles and tear into the cane fields with my BMX bike in search of adventure and other cool things to do. If Huckleberry Finn had a twin sister, it would most definitely be me. The most common conversations and hiding sessions between my mom and I always started with her asking, "Where have you been?" I felt like there was no break. I was not one to stay cooped up in the house. I wanted to be out there, running, riding, laughing, exploring and living.

Instead of playing with dolls and hopscotch with other kids, my curiosity took me to unchartered territories like surreptitious weekend visits to the dwellings of AmaMpondo from the southern coastal belt of Transkei who worked on my dad's sugar cane farm. They worked with and for AmaZulu. From the way they spoke and dressed, you would have thought they came from a different country altogether. Even their gaze bore apprehension and telling. They called this place Mdilova for Mid-Illovo. An ancient name. They also had intense features drawn on their black toned skins—I had never seen people with facial incisions and tattoos until I came closer. I also learned of their kind-hearted nature, which was hard to detect if you caught them arguing or during some rituals.

Legend has it that the relationship between the AmaMpondo and AmaZulu had always been on life support after Shaka's historical warfare on them produced carnage. Although he conquered them, most escaped and the king of AmaZulu is said to have stood on a big rock in the middle of the Umzimvubu River and, for the first time, declared them true warriors.

The Zulus from these shores were tauntingly called AmaMpondo by the Zulus of other regions because of their proximity to this land. Another tribal war must have furthered this intolerance. It broke out on Christmas Eve of 1985 leaving over 150 people dead in just a month. Sources believe that the bloodbath started over land and resource shortages after the influx of AmaMpondo from the Transkei. Many fled the area after torching their own homes, preferring to leave their squatter camps in ashes after the invasions.

Before then, their lodgings were vibrant with song and culture. With no children in sight since their existence here was purely for work reasons. They almost killed me with love and bountiful meat. They also had an organised stokvel culture of selling food and drinks where patrons met and clubbed together to support the host. The mystical singing and whirlwind dancing that would follow in the golden hours of a summer afternoon raised an explosion of awe and wonder in my chest. Unlike most tribes who performed traditional dancing by lifting their feet to the sky and stomping the ground, raising dust, AmaMpondo proudly shook their bodies and processed the songs with their arms, legs, waists and shaking theatrics. They accentuated the dance style with freestyle moves such as war cries and sudden falls. I marvelled at their celebration of life. It was a thing of beauty—what a show!

Of course, come time for refreshments, they would offer me food in serving dishes that would most definitely get me more lashings from my hygiene stringent nurse mom. Honestly, I was seldom hungry, but it would have been rude of me not to eat, so I would gobble the food down, knowing very well that when dusk arrived, I would have to sprint home to face the questions: "Where have you been? Who did you tell?" I paid dearly for my disappearances with hidings. What mattered was that it had been a jol. You have to trade for some of these experiences.

Other times, I hung out at my dad's store where he remarked about my distinction with numbers. I read somewhere that children show symbolic signs to parents from an early age about what they will be when they grow up. Somehow, at the age of ten, and upon hearing this confirmation from father, I appointed myself as the unpaid sugar cane farm depot manager. I would spend the entire weekend recording collections and deliveries, stipulating times, car registrations, drivers' names and so forth. That's the definition of Accountancy, although I didn't know it back then. I just thoroughly enjoyed feeling important by having things on record and thinking someone might need the information one day.

I had a few friends at school, but Faith Nduli was my best friend. We must have been around age six when we first met and we were a curious pair according to onlookers. She had an amputated arm from a bus accident. How they managed to remove her arm but leave a bone attached to what used to be her forearm is inconceivable. I don't think she was even compensated by the bus company or the Road Accident Fund. Many kids stayed away from her, fearing this ghastly elbow. You couldn't recognize this from her animated personality. She was a bubbly girl. I took her into my heart thinking, "So what should happen to this poor girl? She never asked for the accident, and she didn't perform this awful operation on her arm."

Faith and I had a lot of fun, but she often used that elbow against me, threatening to poke me with it whenever we disagreed. She would chase me with it, pointing it at me until I wailed with tears running down my cheeks. Other kids would run after us enjoying the frenzy. Once cornered, she would make dangerous swipes and have me on my knees begging for mercy. One kid would have enough sense to call Nozipho to my rescue whenever this happened. She would say, "Come on. Let me beat her up for you." Yet I was always the first to say no. Not even once did I consider a beat down as suggested. The friendship continued, as sick as it was.

At home, Nozipho was truly my best friend. I followed her everywhere. It must be hard being an older sister. She wasn't without her own flaws. She had her twisted ways that warranted adult intervention, but I was loyal. What would I be without her? One time, after our mother found a stash of sweets that we had stolen from my father's shop, Nozipho made a deal with me for us to turn into "State witnesses" by confessing to the crime. Upon questioning by mom later, and after I had duly confessed to the crime, that girl denied anything to do with the sweets! Needless to say, I took the hiding alone. I don't know where my mom found the time to give us so many lashings. My sister also had this mean, ongoing thing of complete mind puppet mastering. She would give a stellar sudden death performance that was so believable I would cry and cry, mourning her death. She would then proceed to be a ghost that haunted me viciously. You best believe that I also bought her ghost story and progressed to sobbing, utterly defeated. I couldn't report this because once the act was dumped, life resumed to normalcy again. Besides, my mom would have beat the living daylights out of her, so she would beg me not to report her mean games and I obliged.

My brother was also another rascal. Before the killing of my dad and his subsequent killing mission, he was just another tall boy with a leather cap as was the trend of the time. He was naughty as hell. After stealing a pellet rifle, he performed target practice on us to perfect his shooting skill. One day he hit me on my thigh, and I hid the injury until it got septic. I agreed to hide it to protect him until I realised the wound was getting worse. We all got a hiding and I still felt bad for him.

I took no prisoners when it came to my school life though. I was an A student and soared fiercely, sometimes skipping grades because of my high marks. In fact, I was not even a teenager when I enrolled at Lugobe High school. I did my thing there too, scooping all the academic prizes. If someone thought my family kept a success python, my academic achievements would have cemented the suspicion. I had a sharp mind.

That was until a boy called Patrick Ngcongo entered the picture. He disturbed me greatly when he gave me my first academic challenge. The first time it happened, I was shocked but soon put it down to chance on his part. Little did I know that I had met my match. Soon, our names ran simultaneously as we always appeared neck and neck whenever exam results were released. Because the department of education back then made calculations for all subjects, it did not reduce percentages to symbols. You were either number one or number two. Full stop.

Naturally, my favourite subject became Accounting. Despite now having an unwanted academic twin, I had an unwavering belief that I was going somewhere in life. With motivation and the ambition for cars and big houses, I was able to make Patrick eat dust now and then, especially in accounting. It was, however, a new challenge. After humiliating me with the taste of second position, most people thought Patrick and I would be archenemies, but we became friends. I learnt that Patrick had a twin brother named Robert and that they were homeless.

Patrick told me they lived in a trench that they sealed with a makeshift roof at night. He actually took me to the place in question. Although no interview took place about how they found themselves in this situation, I suspect it had a lot to do with the political volatility of the time, which left many children homeless and without relatives willing to take the risk of accommodating them out of fear of revenge from their enemies. I don't know what they ate or how they took a bath. Perhaps they used the school's ablutions and went to the trench to sleep.

I went running to my mom asking her to allow them to stay with us seeing as we already shared our home with so many people. Honestly, I don't remember how that conversation panned out. I just remember that she allowed me to carry food to school for them every day. That was until the night of the arson. I never saw them after that as we started school in Lamontville.

Ask any child, their high school friends live forever in their heads. Some go as far back as primary school. Your friends can sometimes take priority over your relatives, sometimes even your siblings. So, Faith and Patrick continued to live in my head for decades. I tried looking for them especially because I had hoped Patrick would receive an Anglo-American bursary, for which we were both earmarked, but all my attempts drew a blank. I hope to God that life has been kinder to them.

HIGHER LEARNING

I am a very decisive person, not hasty, but I do not procrastinate. From an early age, I have been one who looks at issues, decides and acts upon those resolutions. Therefore, resolving to study towards a degree in Accounting came very easily. First, I had to finish school. Because of the turmoil that followed the burning down of our home and my dad's businesses, my siblings and I lagged in school. We sometimes had to study at home alright, but we needed to write national exams for Matric. We arranged for me to attend Durban Day School, a private school, just to write the Matric exam. I had wasted the previous year moving from here to there and I could not write. Waste a year and you will know the value of time.

By this time, I was 17, having lost an entire year migrating from one place to another, and the need to finish school washed away all anxieties of becoming popular. I applied myself to my studies and really did what I had to do so I could obtain that certificate that would open doors to higher learning institutions.

After Matric, I enrolled for a Diploma in Accounting at the Durban University of Technology (DUT) formerly known as M.L Sultan Technikon. It was a grand establishment with an air of fortitude and freedom. We had smart lecture rooms, a clinic, a library filled to the brim with books, a gym, and labs—the works! I also acquired two friends there, Nomhle Nguzulwana and Vivian (whose surname now escapes me). We all enrolled at the same time. Reality struck when I met students who were repeating a year. The first year - for that matter - for some. They were miserable.

There were benches under the cool shade near the main entrance garden for everyone's use. This meant you could sit and watch people come in and out for the entire day if you chose to. Students also allowed themselves to lounge at the canteen for hours on end. There was no lecturer to run after anyone, you only had yourself to answer to or you could hire a cameraman to immortalise the moment.

M.L Sultan also carried a fashion legacy that influenced even the most conservative students. It was amazing. The style influences at the time were Basketball, Hip Hop and music videos. Most frequented were the surrounding local fashion capitals like the Wheel, The Workshop and the Pavilion in search of oversized t-shirts, baggy jeans and caps. For those with a more discerning taste largely influenced by movies, their fashion was Italian fabrics and flashy jewellery. The retail industry used this to its advantage and lured many students into opening clothing accounts at shops like Edgars, Truworths and Foschini. Jewellery, shoes, jeans, t-shirts, and gym regalia were all highly prized fashion items.

Hair was another area of national importance. Unless it was on point, you were just another farm girl and that's what many student loans paid for.

All this image mania saw students starting their lives on a negative footing of debts that they had to settle with their little internship stipends on top of paying back their student loans.

Student events commenced from the first few weeks of registration. M.L Sultan had its opening parties on the two campuses, Brickfield in Overport and Hertine Court in Albert Park. The roaring parties would be followed by the neighbouring Natal Technikon and Durban Westville's own grandiose events featuring DJs who were big radio names like Bob Mabena and Glen Lewis. Top acts like Thebe, Boom Shaka and Trompies were also headliners at these parties, which were attended by Durban's finest and roughest alike. Mangosuthu Technikon followed suit with their festive soccer tournaments. Soon there were beauty pageants and so it went.

Meanwhile, back on campus, lecture rooms were in full swing. Lecturers continued with their job of lecturing and dishing out assignments while other students occupied their time with their social lives.

Had we been privy to the values that underpinned the Technikon, I am sure most of us would have kept our noses in the books. My research reveals that the institution started as a college in 1957 and was converted into a Technikon in 1984. The founder, M.L Sultan came from India and was trying to make his way to Ceylon when, due to ship mishaps, he ended up heading to South Africa in search of the proverbial greener pastures. He found himself a job as a porter at the Berea Road Train Station in Durban where he met many important, connected and wealthy acquaintances. He later relocated to the Transvaal where he worked as a waiter at the Masonic Hotel. Here, he earned his stripes as a very popular employee due to his fine character.

After venturing into farming tobacco and fruit, Sultan went into retail and wholesale. His success saw him investing in property and establishing a soft goods business known as M.L Sultan and Son. With his business doing well, he ventured into the real estate market, and later owned several properties around the province. In 1941 he was able to pledge a sum of 33 000 pounds towards the establishment of the College, the first institution of its kind for people of colour in South Africa. That college would later become M.L Sultan Technikon.

With this new life requiring so much energy, I was glad for my reclusive personality. Since the days of displacement, I never found a strong foothold for socialising. I was what many call a bird with a broken wing. In fact, all the razzmatazz made me want to finish the task at hand and run away from it all. It was as if I was in my own cold zone while my peers enjoyed their lives and defied the big: "future" talk. It isn't always guaranteed of course but I also believe that when we put our best foot forward, we give the universe no other choice but to propel things along for us.

Then Lady Luck came knocking in my third and final year. I became a recipient of the Mondi London student exchange programme. To qualify, you needed to have passed with flying colours, which I had, both in Matric and at the Technikon. If pride had a face, it was my mom's. She was beaming at that airport. So, off to London I went, leaving my heart behind. I had met my first boyfriend by now and things were going well despite mah not warming up to the idea.

I was placed in a nice apartment in the province of Surrey in Southeast England, which borders Kent to the east, East Sussex to the southeast, West Sussex to the south, and Hampshire to the west. Locals called this the Surrey of Natural Beauty and it was. The landscape is awesome, and the architecture inspiring. The lifestyle is quite slow-paced until a football match is underway. Then it becomes a case of, "who let the dogs out!" Those people are soccer fanatics. I wish I still lived there just for this one aspect of life. So sports-crazy are they that Surrey had its own soccer, rugby and cricket clubs, and every sport exhibited high levels of excitement. However, my apartment was right next to an old-age home, and you don't want to wake the neighbours up with the exhilaration.

I lived on McDonald's meals because, despite the beauty of the land and their roving shopping centres, I found that the British food was not to my liking. I was a child, hardly 21. I think I would have appreciated this opportunity more had I received it at a more mature age. My measurement of a good life involved a lot of fun, outings, great food and such.

At the office, I made myself useful and took in as much of the experience as I could, but I knew from the onset I was only doing this for my CV. I did not intend to stay beyond the stipulated timeframe despite Mondi paying me so well. I was homesick and called home almost every day. I missed my mom and her food. I also missed my boyfriend and my siblings. It was hard.

I managed to stay a year and came out alive. When I received the offer of a full-time job, I had to decline but they were kind enough to employ me in the Durban offices of Mondi. When I returned, I had saved so much money I managed to buy myself a BMW 325i which got me rueful stares from men who saw this as a direct challenge to them. Those who didn't, high fived and praised me for my bravery. It was a popular choice with thugs who always used that make as the getaway car in criminal activities, which meant it was hot property. I was dating a cop. So, when I encountered them I would think, "Let's see one try his luck!" I enjoyed that car, it was a mini beast on the road and a step forward as it meant I didn't have to depend on my mom for transport anymore.

I had intentions to enroll at a Chartered Accounting Institute where I would have been required to first obtain a BCom degree. I didn't mind. Trouble started when I enquired about the market salary. I knew that, in that job, I would be looking at the books and thinking about the remuneration and all joy would flow out of the window. I had not expended so much of my energy for peanuts. At the rate I was to begin, I realised it would take a miracle to take me to where I wanted to be. I was not a person of wonders. I work pretty much in a culture of meritocracy.

Crunching numbers was the easiest part. There were two board exams to go through first. The first one is the Initial Test of Competence (ITC). You are eligible to write it in the year after you pass your Cumulative Translation Adjustment (CTA). Universities prepare you for ITC through CTA. The second exam is the Assessment of Professional Competence (APC). You become eligible after completing 18 months of your training contract.

After completing your learnership and passing both parts of the board exams, you will qualify as a registered Chartered Accountant in South Africa, CA(SA).

My mind began to return to factory settings. I was all for education, but it seemed absurd that I was training so hard with so much of my parents' money, only to end up working for someone else. Numbers are numbers. It's not as if we are talking about medicine where bodies are never the same based on factors like age, gender and health history.

In addition, with the advancement of technology, there were courses I knew would be redundant in due time. The more I thought about it, the more it made sense to be proactive. I developed all these thoughts while I was working as an assistant bookkeeper at Mondi SA. They paid me well there too. So well, in fact, that I was able to pay a portion of my mother's household expenses with my very first salary.

However, a shift happens in a young South African's life when that first salary lands in their bank account. First, you are elated, and then three weeks later you panic. Especially when you are just starting out. This is because of the structure of our economy; you suddenly get anxious that you might not be able to achieve your dreams without doing something drastic to expand your income. It's even worse when you start spending money on the necessities like buying yourself a car or investing in property. You suddenly realise that your dreams do not match your salary and that you might have to stay in a certain bracket for the rest of your life because soon, that car will wear off and need replacing. When you get a place to live, it soon becomes small with the things you buy to furnish it, and so it goes. When do you get to save?

There's also something toxic about a job that gives insight into the company's millions while you are battling your own financial ambitions in your head. It's bound to drive people into depression and even crime. I decided to get myself off the psychological noose by looking for other avenues to help me count and account for my millions. Inevitably, I left the job as soon as I discovered I was pregnant. People said it must have been the pregnancy hormones, but I was not putting my unborn child through that venomousness. I handed in my resignation letter and set about getting myself into business.

I registered a business and looked for contracts and tenders advertised in Government Gazette's Tender Bulletin section. This is not as easy as it seems. You have to be patient and thorough when you apply for a contract or a tender. The procurement procedure requires that you produce the following:

- Certified copy of Company Registration Document that reflects Company Name, Registration number, date of registration and active Directors or Members.
- Certified copy of Shareholders' certificates.
- Certified copy of ID documents of the Directors or Members.
- Last three years audited/reviewed financial statements.
- Letter of guarantee from a registered Financial Institution or Financier covering 3 months' operational costs according to the proposed costs of the bidder.
- Stamped bank letter proving ownership of bank account.
- Proof of Public Indemnity Cover for a minimum of R1 million.
- Letter of Good Standing with the Department of Labour for Unemployment Insurance Fund.
- Letter of Good Standing with the Department of Labour for Compensation of Occupational Injuries and Diseases.
- Proof of compliance/registration with the Industry Regulator / Association.

Government tenders are slightly different in that over and above the list above you have to fill out different documents such as the Standard Bidding Documents (SBD) known as SBD4, SBD6, SBD8 and SBD9. All these are to alert the procurement office of your interest in the tender, score points, qualifications, declare your compliance etc. All this paperwork can keep you busy for a good week or more. Note that this is only to get the procurement officer to consider your company for a pitching session. With some important documents like the Broad-Based Black Economic Empowerment certificate (B-BBEE) only valid for twelve months, you are back to square one if that tender application falls through, a year later, due to the expiry of the B-BBEE certificate. This is where some people close shop and go looking for a nine-to-five job.

MY WORLD

Florah Mkhize

Mama was far ahead of her time. Here she is pictured doing business in various roles including her departure at the airport on route to one of her many international trips.

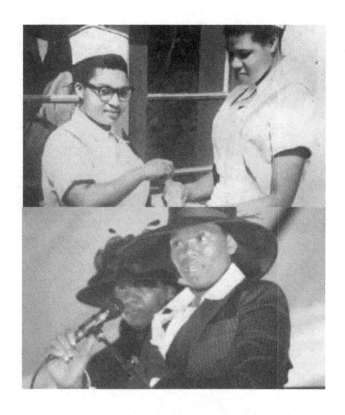

1. A friend of Mama's with Mama on the right at Mc Cords Hospital
2. Shauwn and Nozipho at Mama's funeral

(From left to right)

1. Thabile Zuma, (Sbu's girlfriend) Shauwn & Nozipho
2. Shauwn & Nozipho after Nozipho's graduation
3. Mama with a neighbour at the graduation celebration.
4. Kenneth Mkhize, my father's brother arriving at Nozipho's graduation with Shauwn leading him inside the venue

1. Shauwn, Sphelele, S'bu and Nozipho. Sitting on her own is Fikisiwe Sibisi, our helper at home. **2.** Isipingo shoot out where S'bu ended his life.

1. Sphelele with Nozipho at her graduation.
2. Shauwn with Nozipho at the University of Transkei Res.
3. S'bahle with Shauwn after her accident.
4. Shauwn, S'bahle and Thobeka Madiba Zuma.

(From left to right)

1. Andile visiting S'bahle after her memory had returned.
2. Shauwn as a bridesmaid at Nozipho's wedding.

MY RULES

Andile Mpisane

BIG MONEY AND BIGGER PROBLEMS

The first two years of my business life were the hardest. The first was an illusion. It got me thinking I was finally getting somewhere, only to turn on me. So hard was the second year that instead of making money, I got my name in the worst book known to man. My name was listed on the credit bureau. This meant that I did not qualify for credit. How was I to survive this business life without a backup plan? Once your name was in that dreadful book, it didn't matter if you suddenly raised funds to pay your debts. Your name remained engraved on the credit bureau like a tombstone for a good five years.

While many people battled this draconian punishment, there was a mushrooming of law firms that claimed to have magical manoeuvring skills to remove people from the credit bureau—a blatant and callous scam that saw them spending their last in the hope to replenish their credit worthiness. You were automatically removed from the black book when your time came, which was usually after five years. Unfortunately, many learnt this the hard way.

Those who opted for nine to five jobs to replenish their losses found that they were not employable. A clean credit record is essential when job-hunting. Why would people want jobs if they didn't need them?

Much later, after the Department of Trade, Industry and Competition established a National Credit Regulator to assist consumers to stay out of the credit bureau's bad books, there was a litany of law firms purporting to help people consolidate their debt and pay whatever little they could afford. This is called debt counselling although I have not heard of one person receiving the counselling they so needed. The problem is that the solution is not cheap and it can set a consumer back a few thousand rands that run concurrently with the pennies they shell out to creditors. Meanwhile, the interest is exorbitant for these agreements. In addition, very few creditors will touch you after you enter into this agreement.

My first contract was a renovation project for a township school. We painted and refurbished walls, replaced broken windows, fixed out-of-order toilets etc. Under the apartheid government, children and their well-being were the last thing on the minds of officials. You had to visit these buildings to see the amount of neglect. Judging from the damage and graffiti on school property, the pupils themselves were traumatised. From the walls, and desks, to vandalism in the toilets and libraries - it was obvious. Change was long overdue.

Teachers had their struggles too. Until they formed a Union, the South African Democratic Teachers Union (SADTU), they earned a pittance, which sent them to loan sharks and a life of despair. Under the democratic dispensation, schools were being refurbished, teachers' salaries improved and there was an air of renewal all around. It was a good time to be alive.

Education was at the heart of the new government's agenda, supplying children with free stationery and sowing good vibes around. It was beautiful to be surrounded by beaming faces and bright smiles. I particularly loved viewing the before and after photos. I was proud to be involved in a project that changed the way children saw themselves. There is a Zulu proverb that says, "Lugotshwa lusemanzi." Which means to bend the stick while it's still wet. Figuratively, it means guidance ought to be given at an early age. If children see in action that they have a government that cares for them, they invariably care for themselves and that which belongs to them. The outcome of this is invested citizens. We can only instil these values when the kids are young. To this day, it warms my heart to drive past life-changing projects I have participated in.

Yet because I am a big dreamer, the money earned here just didn't seem enough to give me contentment. Yes, I was already the epitome of success, but I wanted to accumulate sustainable wealth. Life had taught me that money was unpredictable. I was prone to financial anxiety and wanted to bank as much as I could so I could weather the storm if life threw me a curve ball as it did to my family all those many years ago.

I then decided to expand my company's portfolio into food supply for the government-funded feeding schemes in schools. Here was another area of festering sores - hunger in children. Under the old regime, children walked long distances to school on empty stomachs and it was acceptable. Most went back to empty pots in the evenings until an adult could make a plan. Most of those adults were grannies left to look after those children because HIV and Aids had wiped out parents in most households.

I did the paperwork, applied and waited. I was awarded the tender. I started working with cash from my own pocket. The client did not give you capital to commence work; you received payment later. Three months later if you were lucky. So, you would simply carry on. Most often, you received payment six months later. Long after you exhausted your funds and sometimes relationships. This was not only detrimental to your spirit and company profile, but people like me are still paying dearly for this negligence. After exhausting my entire savings running the feeding scheme, holes started appearing in my banking profile. Soon, this plunged my credit rating down the drain and subsequently led to my blacklisting. This is a very tragic experience for someone entering the world of business. Moreover, I was pregnant. Then I had to do the most unthinkable; I had to pawn my BMW-7 Series. The pawnshop owner hit me with 10 per cent interest. These days interest can go as high as 40 per cent.

This reduced me to driving my mom's bakkie with windscreen wipers that had long retired. I drove around with a raw potato to use on my window on rainy days. That year broke the record for the number of days it rained. Do not think for a second that the banks gave me any reprieve since I was already bankrupt. They kept calling. There was a time when I completely avoided calls from withheld numbers just to keep my blood pressure in equilibrium. In essence, I was just postponing the distress because banks have a policy to chase you to your grave and beyond.

With the due date soon approaching for the birth of my baby, I couldn't cower and cry tears. I had the highest hopes for him. I decided to use the loan from the pawnshop to start my own loan scheme business because desperate measures are sometimes all you have. I would keep clients' ATM cards and take my money the minute they were paid. However, when people have a long service in financial struggles, they also tend to dig deeper into their bag of tricks. They left me holding the cards because they went to their banks and simply asked for new ones. Since this business was just a hustle, I had no legal leg to stand on.

I had to change my strategy and swiftly set my eyes on the construction industry. Nothing will push you more than expecting a baby. I'm sure some would like to believe that I went to the department of housing's procurement offices and shouted my surname to miraculously open doors for myself but nope; that history has not been documented. In municipal offices, where I started knocking on doors, they would laugh at me and say, "Go and partner with established companies!"

I had to stalk the procurement office just so they could see my business proposal. It took days and probably my sweet smile to have someone listen to me and hear my story. Procurement offices are hostile. Most offices were run by men, and they didn't like the idea of women in big business. Through their incubation project, I finally and luckily received a small portion to build just 20 RDP houses in Umlazi.

All was going well until my bakkie was stolen. Who steals a pregnant woman's old bakkie though? Even then, I refused to give in. My mom didn't raise a wimp. There was no thinking twice about what I had to do so I went out on a new warpath looking for my mother's old van until I found it. Through the relations I had forged with local street heroes, I only had to say my van was missing before they delivered it to me days later. I had my eyes out everywhere, not relying on street knights to deliver it, and I continued with my life, driving it and building houses until I completed my work there.

MY PHANTOM FAIRY TALE

Obviously, because of the kind of life I lived, I was a late bloomer in relationship matters. Between being ferried to and from school and later work, by my mom come rain or shine, there was very little opportunity for meeting people. Not that I was itching to do so, but that was the nature of my life. After deciding not to follow through with the Chartered Accountant's (CA) qualification, my life became about going to work, working, getting back home, cooking and going to bed before waking up again to prepare for going to work. It was the only life I knew and really, I didn't know if I was missing out on much. I was only too happy for the stability in my life.

Meanwhile, the universe had other plans. One fateful day, mom told me to use public transport, as she was unable to fetch me. I took a minibus taxi, and it was such an awkward moment because I didn't know that passengers had to shout to alert the driver when they wanted to get off closer to their destination. Additionally, I am a soft-spoken person so I was embarrassed picturing myself shouting at the driver as I approached my preferred stop. I asked a guy sitting in the seat in front of me to convey my stop to the driver. When the taxi stopped, I got off and this tall stranger, the one I had asked to convey my stop, got off with me. His name was Sbu Mpisane, and he walked me home. That was the beginning of my first romantic relationship ever, at the age of 19.

It was his height that first attracted me to him. He was also handsome and confident. I might not have dated before, but I knew what I wanted. I did not know much about love, but I knew that I loved the romance and was an affectionate partner. It was most intriguing that I was able to love someone on the level I did. You also have to understand that I came from a place of seclusion. So secluded, in fact, that I found it natural to give a stranger a false name for safety reasons. My sister did the same. Therefore, for a while, Sbu knew me by a different name but understood later when I explained my reasons.

It finally made sense why people did the things they did for love. I would be lying if I said it was love at first sight though. In the initial stages, I particularly loved the thrill of daring and escaping my mom's grip and being in my own world in the company of someone of my choosing. It was not easy. My mom would beat me up because she was against the relationship. Nozipho was not exempted from mom's rule. Even though she met her husband when she was 19, she only received permission to marry him when she turned 25. Thus, when the student exchange opportunity came up, no one was happier than my mom was. It meant she only had one young woman to zoom her eye in on. Poor mom thought we were going to be kids forever.

My love for Sbu grew as we started going out on dates. We dated for a good ten years before I was ready to exchange vows. It seemed that despite his willingness to settle down, his actions defied him. I am sure he really wanted to marry me, although it was evident from the number of occasions I caught him cheating that he would have preferred a marriage that would allow him to see other women. The solution for most men with such desires is polygamy and since I don't see myself in that cultural practice, he must have been at odds. Most Zulu people consider cheating as part of a Zulu man's nature and sanitise it with marriage.

I respect those who see the reason in this culture, but I beg to be excused. I don't even like the way polygamy is so glorified as a new world order or how it's made to look like nature dictates it. Some social 'experts' will ask you to look at the gender ratio to justify this belief. Now you have young girls who proudly enter polygamy as if there is some honour in it.

It took much redemption on Sbu's side for me to agree to marry him eventually, and all against my mother's wishes. My mom reminded me constantly that most women married for sanctuary, even though most ironically end up being breadwinners. That was the general reason. "Most women, all over the world, marry for security but here you are, an empowered woman with everything going for her, wanting to get married! What could possibly be your reason?" she enquired in despair.

She had all evidence of my net worth in the palm of her hands because we were partners in her company, Zikhulise Group from when I turned 22. According to my mom, above all else, women had to benefit from the marriage and not bring financial deliverance to their spouses. I had no time to assess what my reason was so, as you can imagine, it quickly became a sore point. To me, marriage was inevitable. It was a way of life. I knew what I wouldn't marry for, and there was a litany of reasons. I do agree that your options are sometimes as good as your pockets. In hindsight, my mom's notion made sense but back then, I was marrying for love.

If I were to be honest with myself, though, I wanted to marry for the wedding dress! I wanted to walk down the aisle in a beautiful gown in full view of friends and foes. Which girl did not spend her life dreaming of her wedding day? I was no exception. Why? I had seen many power couples working out just fine and building empires as units. Even my parents married for love. Why couldn't I also have it all?

As time ground on, my reasons improved. I wanted my child to be raised by both his parents under the same roof with shared values. At the end of the day, marriage isn't just about comforts. It is not traditionally meant to be an institution that dictates who winds up changing his or her social standing. Hence the vows. Marriage is also a building block within a community structure. My mother, who by now had accepted my relationship with Sbu after I sat her down and spoke firmly to her, was also there to witness the wedding arrangements.

We soon followed the due processes. The ilobolo negotiations were put in place and once the families agreed on the bride price, it was time to get down to the business of planning my fairy-tale wedding. Arrangements for both traditional and white weddings were soon underway.

It was a weeklong affair held at the Zimbali Lodge because we decided to do everything on a grand scale. There was the traditional wedding requiring its various layers of festivity. As with most cultures, there are different stages in a Zulu wedding. The first one is the payment of ilobolo, followed by izibizo, where the groom's family present gifts to that of the bride, followed by umbondo where the bride reciprocates this sharing practice by buying gifts for the groom's family, and then finally, the actual wedding.

To round it off, we had the white wedding, but not before the bridal shower. I have no idea how we managed to keep the madness in check by only having 150 guests. Otherwise, it would have spilled into a pandemonium. I wonder how many people were hurt by this decision. We are a wedding-crazy nation bound to hurt one or a few people by excluding them from the guest list.

Despite the stigma of the yellow dress, I decided to make it a showstopper. Many brides and religious communities scoffed upon the yellow dress as it was reserved for deflowered brides. It was an open admission to your church and community that not only were you "impure", but you also came into the marriage bearing a child. It didn't matter if the groom himself had sired that child. The things we women have been through! These days, even divorcees wear a white dress and to top it off, a veil too. Lately, a yellow dress symbolises wit, sense of humour, abundance, happiness, cordiality etc. Armed with this knowledge, I decided I would be my daring self, to stand apart and be the centre of attention for just one day.

Accordingly, I was adorned with a fitting bouquet. The history of the bouquet is interesting. Folklore says that it was not just an accessory; it had a purpose. The practice of brides carrying bouquets dates to the Ancient Greeks, Romans and Egyptians. Carrying fragrant herbs and spices was meant to ward off bad luck during weddings. The flowers symbolised a new beginning and brought hopes of fertility, happiness, and fidelity. A part of this history even points to hygiene, where herbs and fragrant flowers warded off smells from the bride. We truly have been through a lot as women. Thank heavens this practice is now not more than just a finishing and fun piece.

For the greater part of my marriage to Sbu, I was happy. I felt loved. Moreover, we were very compatible; we were best buddies. So effortless it was to get along that I believed we were made for each other. Of course, neither of us was perfect but I always understood marriage, like all important relationships, to be a trial-and-error journey. The important factor is happiness. I loved my wifely role and embraced it by being a hands-on and obedient wife who treated her family to great bolognaise meals, birthday parties, holidays and entertaining of in-laws and guests. I always strived for great family life. It was a beautiful time.

Then came the tax problems that saw us in and out of court for a good 20 years. With business on the rise, I also found I had more corporate and social responsibilities and new business ventures to attend to, which left me with little time to keep a close eye on my husband. But honestly, why did I have to? I did not think I would have to micromanage someone who knew the meaning of marriage and the vows he made in front of so many witnesses and God without a gun to his head. I had honestly believed we had a great marriage despite occasional turbulences. Even when we celebrated that epic 10th-anniversary marriage in 2011, I still believed I was joyful in my marriage.

That's the reason it took me 25 years to realise there was only one benefactor and one beneficiary in this imagined romance. He was the one lavished with all the love to his heart's content. Do you know the feeling when you suddenly feel exposed, unprotected and naked? You might not even be keeping tabs or analysing the relationship, but the feeling of neglect follows you around. It was as if Cupid had gone on strike. I started feeling that I was just making do; that he left me without my ration of love and romance. There must have been a reason or reasons. Tired of wondering and speculating, I decided to act. Overthinking matters can wreck a good thing. Ignoring glaring facts can also ruin your self-esteem. That is no way to live. I hired a private investigator (PI).

I am a practical person. I wasn't going to put him under the spotlight and ask him to defend himself. That is so pointless. I wanted the kind of evidence that would be so watertight and indefensible it would destroy any soft spot I still had for him. I wanted to have no choice but leave. The PI delivered and the evidence was devastating. So bad that I would not advise this on the faint-hearted, but it worked for me. I had no choice but to walk away.

One of the things I always advise people on the verge of divorce or separation is to strive to remain civil towards each other. Especially when there are children in the equation. I have found that parties cannot be respectful when there are still romantic feelings lurking. Bitterness poisons amity. I have worked at being courteous towards my former husband because I have children with him, I don't ever want them to think of the dissolved marriage as having separated the family into two camps. I have seen it happen in other marriages and it's not a pretty sight.

The media has hounded me to spill the beans and I cannot think of a lower blow than that. I imagine this is the principle that Beyoncé had to apply after that infamous video of her sister Solange, assaulting Jay-Z in a lift. Regardless of the seriousness of the matter, why would anyone want to hang their dirty linen in public? I was raised better than that.

THEN WE WERE FOUR

I fell pregnant before I married my former husband. It was a surprise pregnancy. I had always associated pregnancy with failure. Babies were a drawback because most young women my age had their future stalled by procreation. However, I had to change my attitude fast and be happy with the news. The experience with the all-day sickness wouldn't let me, though. Every smell induced retch. The only thing I liked was that I didn't balloon like most women did. The realisation made me focus more on my plans. I was on my feet all day every day, thinking up better ways to manage my wealth while ensuring I was finding more sources of income.

Expecting Andile became my driving force. I now had someone to be my 100 % responsibility. I had already taken full responsibility for raising S'bahle who came to live with us when she was only ten. Now with two children to feed, clothe, school and raise, I had to charge ahead like a chariot. There was no time to twiddle my thumbs. Of course, Sbu had gainful employment as a traffic officer, but his salary was never going to be enough. My God, I was going to be a mother of two at the age of 25!

Nonetheless, I was glad to learn later that very few mothers will attest to shouldering the task with immediate vigour. The first reaction is shock. Most women say there is never a perfect time to have babies. You are gradually enticed by motherhood by the fact that your body is healthy enough to carry another human being. Then knowing you are never alone for nine months. I have heard that some women abandoned the idea of abortion after they felt the first flutters in their tummies. For others, the pregnancy is a mere existence until they visit their gynaecologist and see the baby's scan or hear the heartbeat. Then it's a whole new ball game. Extremists will start buying baby clothes and paint the baby's room immediately thereafter.

Once you fall in love with your baby bump, so too, comes a flood of unborn baby fears. I am yet to meet a new mother who says they sailed through pregnancy without bouts of anxiety. You wonder, "what if I eat something that kills the baby, what if it's not going to make it? What if I lose my baby at birth or worse, die myself and leave him all by his lonesome self in this cruel, cruel world? Who would raise him?"

My only sense of comfort was from the other mothers I met during visits to the maternity clinic who had similar fears or those who continued as if nothing in their life had changed.

I thank God for the gift of books and technology. Through these, I was able to keep abreast of the developing baby inside of me. I could just focus on feeling this growing tiny body and acknowledge its growth without being overly anxious. With my baby inside of me at a time when I was trying to get a foothold in the world of business and with so many dragons to slay, I felt like we were together in our journeys united by love. I had to carry things through and realise my full potential for his sake.

The moment I learnt of my pregnancy, I kept a record of all the milestones; the first kick of my bump, the foetal developmental stages, his birth, his first smile and such. Yet, I was not an overprotective mother. I kept the baby in his car seat and refused for people to pick him up, fearing he would become accustomed to being held and start demanding it from me. My hands were full trying to get the business to stand on its two feet.

The birth of Andile on 15 March 2000 was unbelievably manageable. Other women in the maternity ward thought I was faking delivery because even with dilation in progress my pain was not as excruciating as theirs despite not taking an epidural. I was not spared the reality of birthing and nurturing an infant though. It's a bittersweet experience. Nausea, that had been so persistent that I thought it was permanent, disappeared the minute the baby was born. What a relief!

In my culture, new mothers - especially first-time mothers - nest with their mothers for the first six weeks. So accordingly, I had to leave the hospital bed and head straight to my mom's house. Reason el primo is that as a woman the father might coerce you to become sexually active before the recuperating six-week window period has passed. It is during this nesting period that a new mother learns how to care for her newborn and herself. It should become a compulsory course.

You learn things like how to care for the umbilical cord, bath the baby and develop routine, especially feeding and sleeping times. You also learn crucial things like burping the baby, keeping his food fresh and soothing him. My mom had become an expert at this with her four children and my sister's two babies.

She adored my baby. Judging by those tiny fingers clamped around hers and those trusting eyes, the feeling was mutual. Babies are precious. What a beautiful feeling it is to watch two people you love with everything in you, look at each other with such love!

Breastfeeding mothers learn to express breast milk and help the baby latch, an agonising experience. In the event of C-sections and episiotomy, the new mother is taught to care for the savage wounds which heal by first inflicting excruciating pain before being unbelievably itchy. Thankfully, my mom - having been a nurse all those many years ago - knew how to make the experience a little easier. So nurturing she was of Andile and I that I dreaded going home, although I was ready to look after my baby on my own by the time I left. I was even able to take the baby to the office and juggle that with the running of my home.

As nature would have it, self-doubt visits now and then when alone with the baby. You have no idea how many gory stories of negative things happening to babies you will remember when you have your baby in your arms. Fears like cot deaths, suffocation by sleeping on the baby, deadly over-feeding, and dropping the baby will haunt you day and night. Let's not forget relatives who suddenly all seem to have an opinion on what's best for your baby. Some crawl out of nowhere to advise on your readiness for another baby and how many to aim for. We come from big families in the Zulu culture, but when you are reluctant to overpopulate, especially the in-laws hold you in contempt. How I managed to hold on to my decision is unbelievable, even to myself.

There is a big difference between women who nurture a newborn with the help of others and those who do it by themselves. Although I was somewhat trained at parenting through the introduction of S'bahle earlier in my life, I had not been prepared for the reality of using one hand to prepare a baby's bottle, while the other held him. In addition, the feeding and changing of nappies were stuff I had not done before. However, the desire to give him a better life raged more than my challenges.

S'bahle, whom I was so sure I had prepared adequately for the arrival of her brother, was not ecstatic at losing her position as the only child. She sulked and darted around the baby, not being fully involved. I thought she would be inseparable from her baby brother. Psychologists call this petulance sibling rivalry. Thankfully, it was short-lived. I don't know how I would have handled that. You really must have your own children to realise how a manual would come in handy at such times...

My boy was a content little man. He was never a fussy baby like some infants I had seen. It was like a reward for that long and taxing journey of pregnancy. I couldn't take my eyes off him. I had finally discovered that grand insurgence of bottomless love I had heard so much about.

We were a perfect family portrait. Now with more people to share my grand love with what more could a mother ask for? Mine was to ensure they were well taken care of. With S'bahle attending St Mary's Diocesan School for Girls, one of the most expensive private schools in South Africa, I focused on caring for the little one. I dressed and fed him well. Nevertheless, being the long-sighted person I was, I always looked at ways to ensure the comforts they enjoyed were not temporary.

It was painful to have to instil tough discipline, especially with S'bahle. She knew I was quick to forgive, so she would dance around precious objects when it was time to get a hiding and that would be the end of the disciplinary mission. Honestly, when it came to Andile, there was never a need to raise the rod. He was always a gentle soul. So gentle in fact, that I feared that he might have inherited my own soft heart. I feared that people would try to take advantage of him. My initial years in business taught me just how easily kind souls can be taken for a ride. I have brought him closer to me, not to cushion him against the cruel world but to give him skills in the school of hard knocks.

On the other hand, there was S'bahle and her tenacity. My immediate nurturing involved striking balance between embracing her independence and giving her support. It is important to remember that children change with the seasons. There was a time I had to get her out of her cocoon but once she came out, I had to create stability and boundaries. Being a mother is not easy.

LOVE IN THE TIMES OF COVID

That one day a child would have its own offspring was unthinkable to me. Inevitable yes, but still an absurd idea until it happened. When does a child grow up and become a father or a mother? Yet, it happened and God's timing could not have been more precise. Baby Flora was born at the time of the COVID-19 pandemic depression and it changed the entire atmosphere in the house.

At the end of 2019, news reports started coming through regarding the discovery of a novel coronavirus in Wuhan, China and the Beijing government instituted an extreme lockdown. When the first case arrived in South Africa on March 05, 2020, we were told of a couple who had been in Italy and quarantined upon arrival in South Africa. Although there were no guarantees, everyone was hopeful those two would not bring further COVID cases into South Africa. The National Institute for Communicable Diseases (NICD) said the couple had been a part of a group of 10 people and had two children. That on its own should have told us we were in for a bumpy ride. But hope sometimes defies logic.

Soon, the NICD reported more cases and when President Cyril Ramaphosa appeared on TV ten days later, as many as 61 people had tested positive for the disease. He placed the Country under lockdown initially for 21 days. The few people we saw, since everyone was to stay home and only visit shopping centres or hospitals for emergencies, walked around in a daze. We had to stand in queues for everything from vitamins to food as only a handful of people could share a certain space at a time.

News bulletins continued to share bad news from all over the world. China and Italy were worse off although America was closing in on the number of deaths. In 1918, history recorded the death of over 20 million people from influenza around the world before the eventual development of a cure. We had to be hopeful that our technology was more advanced than it had been back then. In the meantime, everyone walked around with creased foreheads. Thousands, if not millions of people lost their jobs, and we were living in a completely new world. When the government shut the country down indefinitely and imposed house stay laws, the reality of the pandemic became real.

This would have a devastating effect on the economy, which was already on crutches. Businesses went under, people died, flights grounded, and restaurants and sports activities closed down. Inevitably, the funeral business boomed, and we watched in total disbelief as this "new normal" was imposed on us. South Africa became depressed. We were cold, we wore masks, we couldn't go out and every second news bulletin had a death announcement of someone prominent. The pandemic did not spare us regular citizens. So many people passed on. I lost workers, business associates, friends and relatives to the disease. Anxiety was the order of the day!

Then amid all that depression, baby Flora was born. I could not have asked for a more uplifting mood enhancer. I was neither ready nor prepared but boy, oh boy, I never understood the impact and joy that she would bring into our family. It seems everyone started walking around with smiles and spoke baby talk. Her beautiful presence changed the tone in the house completely. Even the workers had blurred lines with her around. Her mom was so kind to stay with the baby in our home. I would do anything and everything in my power to protect her from this world.

God was not done with his torrential showers of miracles because just as we were counting our blessings and naming them one by one, in came her sister, Coco, a year later. My heart is bursting at the seams because I have never known so much love. When someone changes the entire nature of your day by just looking at you and setting your heart on fire with her smile, it's too much!

I now have my heart completely captured. I might go out with a sword to fight all the dragons, but when I come home, my heart grows and swells. It's a phenomenal feeling. Imagine having a double dosage of that. If I have ever wondered whether I am, I now know, for a fact, that I am blessed. No, triple that.

I was a loving and supporting mother to their dad, alright. Nevertheless, I hold personal testimony that grannies love their grand kids with a staggering, emotional and disarming love we run out of words to describe.

The world found new ways of coping without the workforce, which meant most people's jobs were becoming redundant. As an employer, you want to make a profit, necessary, but I am sure it hurt even the most capitalistic employers to get rid of so many people. Thankfully, I was able to keep most of my workforce.

THE HANGMAN GAME OF TAXMAN

To use Benjamin Franklin's famous quote: "Nothing is certain but death and taxes". No one knows this better than an accountant does. I mean we all know that without citizens paying their taxes, a tradition dating back to 3000BC in Egypt, the state would collapse. So significant and lucrative has tax collection become that the one scripture most churches never forget to preach is the 10 per cent tithe. It's anyone's guess how these institutions get away with not paying taxes seeing as so many South Africans attend church and heed the tithe call.

People have wondered and said so much about me and my relationship with the taxman. For the record - I was sure I was doing everything by the book as far as the South African Revenue Services (SARS) was concerned, but clearly, I was not and when this was revealed, I was shocked. What was interesting about my tax issues is that the officials, on their own accord, did not unearth them. It was a chain of events that led to me being investigated and humiliated in the way that I was. Very much, like the hangman game.

In the wake of my numerous business enterprises with their different profiles, I went to the SARS offices to say: "Here are my books. Scrutinise them and give me advice on how to conduct my tax affairs better if need be." But as was the nature of our lives as the family, it was as if I had done the opposite because that is when SARS took the opportunity to nail me. They ordered the freezing of my bank accounts and the seizure of our cars by the Asset Forfeiture Unit (AFU). The press had a field day.

I doubt people would know me as well as they do now had that tax saga not made such enthralling news headlines. Suddenly, I was thee Shauwn, enemy to the SARS office. Pictures of me and my former husband were splashed like we were celebrities or royalty with a lot to hide.

In hindsight, I should have expected it. The excitement. Most wealthy families are never to be left alone. Some say it comes with the territory. Had the exhilaration of the press been more containable I would have given an interview to give my side of the story but with every report, the story became a case of a broken telephone and it just got out of hand. That car that my former husband drove to work and drew so much attention to himself, did not help either.

The last thing I expected was to be hanged proverbially for declaring my innocence. It reminded me of the time my dad was encouraged to hand himself in by his lawyer, only to wind be up in a ditch, stone cold. Was this really happening? Had I not been through enough trying to break into the business? I thought I had earned my dues and was looking forward to a life of managing my wealth when, out of the blue, my world came crashing down.

The next move was to sit down with my auditor and check what we had done wrong. We had been filing through SARS's system. It was mind-boggling that a system that could calculate a taxpayer's due monies in seconds was unable to do the same with company profiles (Why can't SARS make its calculations of company tax submission the same way it does for individuals?). The only argument given over the years has been that the system depends on declarations, yet they have access to all South African departments and the banks.

Nonetheless, the first trial day was a David versus Goliath battle. I held my head up but inside I was a dark cloud, swirling with heavy rain. My legal team and I had to prove that I had been paying taxes. SARS had to prove otherwise. The court appearance was a session we had prepared weeks in advance for. An awful experience because it's like splitting hairs, trying to find your fault. You have to relook at the facts, and they don't change just because you are being asked to prove them. Those convergences didn't come for free. Faced with the state's most intimidating institution, I had a litany of charges to answer for.

Most allegations levelled against me related to tax evasion. I had been accused of cooking up books to pay less tax. One of the glaring false claims was that I attempted to bribe a witness in a tax matter. Our submissions were prodded, pummelled and thrown about for good measure by people who shopped for new clothes in case they were caught by media cameras.

Concerning the paramount matter, in the submission of evidence from both sides, it was clear that there were records of over and understating of taxes. SARS accused me of owing R4.7 million.

When your assets are seized, you are liable for the rental of their storage. Some charge as much as R1000 per car and with 60 vehicles in forfeiture, I was looking at R60 000 per day. How draconian is this law? However, I was not hit with this additional expense because the forfeiture had been unlawful to begin with.

This did not make my unpleasant journey with SARS any easier. The hours were long, not like the cases on TV. Courts recess and postpone which means you can never confirm your movements until Lord Judge gives you a new date during which you cannot even book a flight from Durban to Johannesburg because who knows what time the court can adjourn? You basically become a walking prisoner. It is not a pleasant experience. It is one of the greatest inconveniences, for which no one reimburses, even if you end up winning the case.

Throughout the first five years of the lawsuit, I attended the proceedings, listened to practitioners battle it out and exchange evidence for and against me. It was exhausting but the interesting aspect of lengthy trials is that once you get over the shock and the mental exhaustion, some words become familiar, and your understanding of the jargon improves. You start comprehending with clearer insight. You also realise the importance of facts as well as how you can fight from behind.

Through gathered facts, specialist prosecutor Meera Naidu was proved to have suppressed all evidence of my innocence and she was taken off the case and served with notice of proposed suspension for the alleged misconduct. Of course, this did not happen overnight. But still, "Boom!"

SARS senior auditor, Waheeda Osman also admitted to "amnesia" over documentation that showed my attempts at compliance. Then Arno Rossouw took over the case as senior state advocate. I was given a tax clearance. This was in 2013. It did not mean all my charges were withdrawn. However, I had done some impressive pushback. Courts are not for the faint-hearted.

With the legal team in possession of strong evidence against the previous SARS auditors, we applied to the National Director of Public Prosecutions Advocate Mxolisi Nxasana to have the case withdrawn over prosecutorial misconduct. This was after months and years of evidence gathering and deliberations. By the way, with a pending case like mine, obtaining any kind of evidence required a rigmarole of processes. Thankfully, we won the case, and all the charges were withdrawn against us. These are the victories or exonerations that were not publicised. The media was decidedly intent on stories that painted us in a certain light. Nonetheless, our assets were also returned after the National Prosecuting Authority's spokesperson, Nathi Ncube said the alleged misconduct by prosecutors, was so serious that to continue with the prosecution would have been a miscarriage of justice. The misconduct, he said, was so bad that "we could not undo the damage". Even that sweeping statement did not see the light of day in the media.

We were elated of course but no one could or would undo the damage caused to us. It left a very bitter taste in the mouth. I lost hundreds of hours, missed important events, and paid dearly, emotionally. In addition, despite the victory, potential clients and the public still largely viewed me as a dubious character. That does a lot of harm to someone's position in the community. Imagine the damage it causes to the children. Even the source of my wealth was now a topic by all and sundry. I was now referred to as a "convicted fraudster", a questionable businesswoman. And this is where I am thankful to God for the personality he gave me. Never once was I so affected that I wanted to hide. I still walked with my chin up high because I believed in my innocence when others did not. Some would give anything to see me hang.

Four years later, SARS accused Zikhulise Group of owing as much as R200 million in tax. Newspaper reports surfaced that we acknowledged the debts but were "not in a position to pay the outstanding tax debt" because government departments had not been paying us. It has always been a well-known fact that the government's late payments have sent many businesses to their knees and in most cases, their graves. How was it reported so flippantly and with such glee that we had been dealt the same fate?

After going through the same ritual of appearing, media chronicals, appealing, and being exonerated again, our assets were returned. That didn't come without an exorbitant emotional price tag either. So affected was I by the experience that the idea of having my cars back was starting to feel like bad deja vu. It gave me bad vibes instead of joy. I decided at this stage that selling the whole lot was the way to go. The idea of them up on a pick-up truck and them back again was just too much to bear. It started to feel like an evil tease. You know the kind where someone takes your valuable item and they watch you look and turn the house upside down looking for it and then when you are ready to just collapse and die, they say, "Here it is. Be careful next time?"

I was better off starting afresh. I felt that all the litigation had contaminated those possessions. I even believed they bore bad luck.

We sadly learnt that even after the extortionate settlement, SARS had been in no hurry in implementing the changes that came with the settlement. It's heart breaking no matter how you look at it. I doubt I would ever make peace with this tax journey; it tainted my mother's company and was a huge financial setback. I always had to remind myself that it's hard to see the reason for the course when still in the eye of the storm. You look around and you wonder how much longer you can continue to hold on. Especially when in the process you find yourself dealing with adversity like theft, dishonesty and late payments.

During an interview with DJ Sbu, he revealed with much banter how he lost his first car to theft outside the SABC studios. But did he give in or wallow in self-pity? Nope. Instead, that man has been on the radio for 20 years. He has created his brand as a philanthropist, businessman, and motivational speaker.

I'm also reminded of the story of a businesswoman who entered into a 24-month lease agreement for a franchise that fell through. She had to continue paying crippling rental for a business that in essence did not exist. This could have been the end of her. But did she commit suicide? Instead, her name is up there with one of South Africa's most successful businesswomen.

These are only two stories of enduring businesspeople who have seen things through. Everywhere I go, black businesspeople have not had it easy. Even in the US, Steve Harvey's tale is not so different from what we go through. He says in 1991, he lived in his car for a year and had sobbed a prayer of giving up when he heard the voice of God saying, "If you get up, I will take you to places you have never been." Because his failures had beaten him down so badly, he says he stood up, thinking "I'm giving up anyway..." not knowing his prayers had been answered. He soon found out. Look at his brand now.

There is nothing easy about negotiating this tightrope. All I know is that you have to keep on going. Draw your strength from wherever you need to because you are going to need to get yourself out of the funk somehow. And because the world of business is rapid, there is no time to sit down and hug yourself or rest on your laurels, it's easy for people to think their struggles are worse or that they warrant giving up or taking their own lives. That is a big mistake. Usually, as was the case with Harvey, a breakthrough is always around the corner. I don't know why the universe waits that long but after rock bottom; the only way is up indeed.

IN A MASTER CLASS OF MY OWN

One could compare my evolution to that of the making of a butterfly, and I have a short story as to why I say so. There is a tale that a compassionate man was waiting for a bus at a bus station and saw not too far from his feet, a ball of cocoon rolling up and down in frustration. However, the bus came before he could see the end of that struggle. The following day he remembered the cocoon and realised in horror and sympathy that the cocoon was still at it pushing this way and that way. He quickly took the cocoon in his hands and decided to help the caterpillar inside by breaking the cocoon open. His bus arrived soon after this act of kindness.

On the third day, he noticed with shock that the butterfly was struggling to take off and fly and on close inspection, he discovered the butterfly had only one developed wing. "You did that to her," said the old man who had witnessed this developing story from day one. "The struggle inside the ball of mud was supposed to help him develop his wings into full ability but you disabled her by breaking the cocoon."

Even as I go through my short spells of resentment at the struggles I have gone through, I realise, they were meant to make me stronger; arm me with the tools and intelligence I would be able to implement into the businesswoman I am today. Develop my professional wing muscles so to speak.

The few lessons I would like to share are as follows:

Positivity: The first thing I chose to do early in life was to be a happy person despite everything. For instance, my parents named me Shauwn because they had expected a boy after my sister Nozipho. There was a nice order before me. First came a boy (S'bu) then a girl (Nozipho) and the pattern was supposed to continue with them having, yes, a boy after Nozipho. But it wasn't to be because, "Boom!" there I was. I was stuck with a boy's name. It was the same with my mom. Her other name was Dumazile (one who disappointed) because her parents were expecting a boy. She lived with that negative name, but did she disappoint herself? Hell no.

My other name is Junior, which when you think about it sounds like a feminist breakthrough. One can argue and say it sounds like an afterthought; a crisis, a "what do we do now?" kind of name. I took it all in my stride and even ditched a third name, Mabongi. I chose to go with my masculine name and play the game of men.

Stand Up Against Injustice: I have been constantly tortured with assumptions that my business growth could not happen without my political affiliations. For a long time I rolled with these punches and after taking these insults, I have learnt to assert, "But I am not alone. There are many other political beneficiaries. What has set me apart is my work ethic and risk-taking abilities."

The three factors that worked for me when I came into the world of business were my youth, my gender and my race. After that, I grabbed opportunities by making sure I did not deliver sub-standard work, to be considered for other projects. I also took on projects that enabled my company to grow in grading. Whereas most remember our company for the construction of RDP houses, we have advanced to bigger projects like the building of schools, clinics and reservoirs.

Principles: When I was 18, my sister encouraged me to join a modelling agency as a way of having some form of social life. Looking back, she was not just throwing me into the deep end to help me to swim. I was tall, lean, dark and pretty with pitch-black hair that was thick and long. Because of childhood trauma, I was too introverted. My sister coerced me into joining a modelling agency. I loved this semi-chapter of my life. It validated something sacred within. I shed off the tomboy tendencies to become a model. Who could have thought? What could be more fantastic than that?

My modelling agent sent me to different clients for castings and a few of them booked me. I would sometimes get to a casting venue and see other beautiful people, models with the brightest smiles and others with the most flawless skins. It was so amazing that these beautiful people lived amongst us. Then there were others with a beauty that was not that vivid but were popular with agents because they were photogenic. Indeed, when you looked at their zap cards, you would think it was a joke. They looked a hundred times better than in real life. Others modelled just their hands or legs. One thing was common, people loved modelling not only for their street cred but for the good money it paid. Big corporate clients like Coke and Vodacom paid the kind of money that allowed models to buy cars for cash and from one cheque.

The biggest modelling gig I ever cast for and won was for a Peter Stuyvesant ad. The one with crowds clad in white having the most fun on a white cruise ship heading into the glorious sunset. I just remember that the amount of money was insane, and I was excited about it. Sadly, I had to decline the offer because it didn't sit well with Sbu. That was the end of that career.

I don't agree with people making moral decisions on behalf of others, but that act was my boon and bane. It made me realise that self-branding requires one to ask oneself ethical questions with every interest. How could I endorse smoking? I was curious about the modelling world. I feel that it was one of those things that were nipped in the bud without my consent. These are the building blocks of reputational management, every business' shield.

Evolution: These are some of the reasons I agreed to the KwaMamkhize reality television show. Contrary to popular belief, it was not a self-indulgent exercise. It might have looked flashy, but it was a rebranding strategy for me as a single businesswoman. It was to reclaim my name, which is so linked to my commercial life. It was a reputational sanitisation exercise. It was to show the world my high work ethic. It didn't hurt that it allowed me to be the new person I discovered I was.

As a businessperson, you are in constant evolution. You win some, you lose some, but you never lose sight of what you are about. One of the decisions that left people stunned is hiring Filipino women as my helpers at home. This had nothing to do with attention seeking. In fact, the decision was quite the opposite. I decided to have people who would take their job seriously. I had learnt over the years that helpers tended to merge themselves into the family. I wanted peace of mind; the kind where I didn't have to ask why something was not done or done a certain way. This again was a painful but necessary decision.

Self-Preservation: When we were growing up in Umbumbulu, ours was the only home with white landscapers. This was not done out of flossing. People who knew much about landscaping did not surround us. Sure, black people can tend the land by farming it but for aesthetics, my dad found he had no choice but to have white landscapers. Of course, people thought he had taken his sense of importance to another level. Now I understand his stance. For your optimum performance, you sometimes must make questionable and uncomfortable decisions. Look at it as an investment in your mental well-being.

I observed that Filipinos were in the hospitality industry all over the world. I gradually learnt their demeanour and commissioned an agent in Dubai to get me three women. They are disciplined, hardworking and give you unpretentious care without getting in your face. They also know when to leave you alone and never get emotionally involved in your family matters. The other trait I particularly liked about them was their cooking culture. They prepare the healthiest everyday food, and this came in handy for me when I went on a weight-loss venture. I have enjoyed adobo, a traditional and very healthy dish of meat, seafood, and vegetables marinated in vinegar, soy sauce, garlic, bay leaves and black peppercorns. It's a meal that might just raise the dead in its fragrance, taste and health properties.

Dreaming Big: I always feign a complaint that my mom left me with too much responsibility. I have an obligation to hold up her name and legacy. Even when I was a partner in her business at 22, she still called the shots. She is the one who decided to start the business. This is why I had two accounting jobs even though I was one of the directors at Zikhulise. I worked for an oil refinery company by day and a strategic financial management company by night as an accountant.

My dreams were huge, and this required my work ethic to be higher. However, I do have fewer demands from the people I hire. All 4500 staff members have different qualities about them, on which the success of my company depends.

I believe that only hard work will produce sweet fruits. No one should ever have to sell their soul to get somewhere in life. Not a woman, not a man, not anyone. One of my biggest hopes for my children and grandchildren is for them to conquer the world without having to deal with the hurdles of being black.

Image Focus: I have often heard that image is everything. Therefore, when I decided to embark on a weight loss journey, I set myself a new goal of healthier eating and general healthy habits. But the Instagram page was nothing I had planned to do. I have to say that it's very encouraging to see the results of my hard work.

THE BUSINESS OF SOCCER

My mom left me with a lot of responsibility when she left Zikhulise in my hands. She passed on in August 2008. It was a company of relative success, but I wanted resounding success for it so maybe in a way I am the one who put pressure on my shoulders, not my mom.

I have blazed a trail where others saw nothing but disaster. I have followed my hunch, sometimes a business idea comes from my research, but no executive decision is a spur-of-the-moment decision. Even when I built houses for my employees, it was both an act of compassion as well as an appreciation for what they had invested in the company. Who wouldn't want to work for such a company?

One such project has been the soccer business, which grew on me. Growing up, all I ever knew were the three giant football clubs: Kaizer Chiefs, Orlando Pirates and Mamelodi Sundowns. That I would one day find myself in this business is a shock to me too. I also have many reminders from men in the business. They seem to have been offended that I am a woman talking men's stuff. They don't even call me by my name, preferring to leave things at "This Woman!" I understand. It was the same when I bought cars that were deemed masculine.

My experience has been bittersweet so far. I was drawn to football after seeing that my son, from a young age, had a passion for the game. I was drawn into it purely by the sheer love of it as well as its addictive qualities. What a lot of fun!

I started as a super fan soccer mom who always ran alongside the touchline cheering my son and his friends on. Even at my busiest, I never missed a game. This interest grew when Andile started playing for AmaZulu under-16 squad. My former husband and I discussed at length the possibility of this investment. That is how we went into founding Royal Eagles. We bought a team known as Sivutsa Stars based in Nelspruit, moved it to Pietermaritzburg, renamed it Royal Eagles and developed it. Sbu was the chair, I was the deputy and Andile was the junior chair.

During the divorce, the soccer club became a bone of contention. It pained me deeply to have to walk away from something I was so instrumental in starting especially because we established it as a legacy for our son. We chose to walk away because inner fighting was not going to serve anyone. It would have been detrimental to the morale of the club since those boys were like my own children. I also decided that we would forge ahead and therefore decided it would be in our interest for Andile and for me not to be seen as aggressive. My dad always said, it didn't matter if you entered through a window or had to break the door down, what mattered is how you conducted yourself once at the table.

The club was still at the Glad Africa Championship level; this is the second-highest division soccer league officially known as National First Division (NFD). This is the leg of progress that graduates the highest and last team standing to the Premier Soccer League (PSL). Every serious soccer team owner wants their team to swim with the sharks of the PSL. We were no exception.

The PSL is a national sports association responsible for administering the two professional football divisions in South Africa: the DStv Premiership and Glad Africa Championships. The South African Premier Division is officially referred to as the DStv Premiership for sponsorship reasons. It is the highest soccer league and the highest division of the South African football league system. As the division is the top level of association football in South Africa, it is sometimes commonly referred to as (PSL) – the name of the country's administrator of professional football.

After losing Royal Eagles, Andile and I went into a think tank and subsequently founded Royal AM from scouting players. Some players deferred to us immediately while some came later to the camp citing contractual obligations. Our mission was to put together a winning team. Thankfully, one of the gifts Andile has is talent scouting. Together we discussed at length general mistakes of other big teams like bringing in big names to their camps only to end up being beaten by smaller teams. I look for hunger and diligence in my players and so far, so good.

With Andile known as the youngest chairman in the PSL and listed as a player for Royal AM in the initial stages, I have had to explain my decisions until I would turn blue in the face. Not every classroom has four walls. I said it was a business decision. It won't help him to only play soccer and not have the knowledge on the administrative side of things. I have backed this decision by hiring experienced coaches in the club. It is good for him to grab knowledge from people who know better. People who have been in the soccer fraternity for quite some time, were players and now work as coaches. Mentoring doesn't get better than that.

Not that the incidents so far have not been enough training ground. One is the most talked-about arbitration by the Court of Arbitration for Sports (CAS). It arose from an unfortunate technicality, and I was not prepared to take it on the chin. What happened was that we played to the top of the Glad Africa Championships, which gave us the promotion to the DStv Premiership League. Then in January 2021, two teams Sekhukhune United and Polokwane City played against each other. It was discovered that Polokwane City had not abided by the Glad Africa law which requires teams in its championships to have five players from the under 23 league. With this, arbitration lawyer, Advocate Hilton Epstein ruled in favour of Sekhukhune United. This automatically took them to the first position of Glad Africa, a position we were already occupying. What followed was confusion. We were billed for playoffs, which we naturally boycotted. Then I was told I was guilty and liable for a fine for "absconding from those games". How unfair! That's like being asked to go for a starter after you have had your dessert.

Even as we continued winning in the DStv Premiership, I had to pay a fine of R4m. I had to negotiate the facts mentioned above until R2.8m of that was suspended. What hurt me the most about this particular marathon was that the PSL had initially disagreed with Epstein's ruling. They had even promised to intervene on my club's behalf. I guess when it came to crunch time, people knew which side their bread was buttered. While they were dilly-dallying, the 21-day appeal period lapsed which also made matters difficult for us. That was the reason for my delay in approaching CAS.

The other burning accusation by people looking from outside is that I spoil my kids. My kids are not spoilt. They are loved and of course, I support their dreams. Having walked the business journey alone, I don't want them to relent or even think about working for someone else. I could never live his life for him, but I choose to hold his hand because I do not want him to walk this journey alone. It's my investment into my legacy too.

After establishing the soccer club, I bought another soccer club with a good footprint, known as Bloemfontein Celtics and we incorporated it into Royal AM. I immediately went into a balls-building mission. Nutrition, the uniform, living conditions and salaries were top of my agenda. You cannot expect excellence where you do not invest. As a result, Royal AM lost only two opening games but turned things around to win four consecutive games after we played six games in the DStv Premiership in 2021. On September 18, 2021, we commanded overdue respect when we beat Kaizer Chiefs 4-1. We trended for a good three days on Twitter with people singing our "Thwihli Thwahla" payoff line, strengthening our confidence to new heights. Unfortunately, for Chiefs, this sent them to a humble number 12 in the league. Most of their fans were seen burning their paraphernalia, it was sad. Meanwhile, we were sitting pretty at number two on the log at the time of writing this book.

The only skill I am to acquire is staying calm through it all. As mentioned earlier, the game of soccer is exhilarating, which means the wins are delirious and the losses humbling.

The rollercoaster that is the game of soccer became vivid when Swallows beat us in our first game. We were sad about two consecutive losses. It was not nice. That is all in a day's work. Sometimes you win and sometimes you lose. Failure forces us to delve deep into our bag of talents and abilities. If you are still alive, you have the chance to try again. Not as a bird with a broken wing but as a champion back to claim what is his.

This is the message I had to sow in all 60 players at my disposal. This amounted to 180 meals a day. One thing about soccer stars - they EAT! Not only are they growing young men but also sportsmen. Until fans were allowed back in the stadiums, this remained one of my financial responsibilities. In January 2022, we sadly had to part ways with 15 players. We also brought in great new players.

These are the reasons for our wild celebrations. We do not mean to offend anyone; they serve as a morale boost for the boys. We used to celebrate that way even when we were at Royal Eagles under Glad Africa Championships. Like most fraternities, the league has controversial regulations and at times, they don't get it right. Neither do I, but I have challenged unjust or unnecessary laws. It gives us both something new to learn. Even the Bible, which is said to have been edited over 200 times, has the Old Testament. Numerous religious scholars have questioned its existence. Nothing is cast in stone. We lost the CAS case sadly, but we continue to win.

OVER THE RAINBOW

Nothing can ever compare to a mother's love. That one person whose voice you first recognise when you are in her tummy. Mum is that one person we trust with all our being and run to in times of happiness and crisis. Her baby stretches its arms towards her without a doubt. Her bosom is the safest place to be in the whole world. Although we never anticipate it, death lingers in the shadows for all of us. You would think we would be better equipped for the eventuality of death, but Africans are particularly terrified of this final chapter of life. My mom the stalwart was not exempt from the theft of life.

After losing our father at such a young age, mah assumed the role of both mother and father with aplomb. She saw us through our triumphs and fears with a steady and sometimes heavy hand when she felt we were drifting towards danger. None wondered just how much her strength would take a toll on her spirit and inevitably her body. We were all too glad to have her alive. Brothers had a sister, cousins had their legendary cousin, comrades had their imbokodo and children had their loving mother. Additionally, the broader community depended on her to change their lives or those of their children.

She became a councillor of Ward 96 Durban after the new dispensation at the age of 52. Ward 96 was a sub-region that encompassed Umbumbulu, with a population of about 32 000 residents according to the 2011 census. It was a ward divided into the slight haves and many have-nots with dire challenges in housing settlements, ablutions, health care, identity registration and a growing HIV rampage amongst other emergencies. All residents here, including people who once considered her the enemy of the people, flooded her offices with requests for service delivery, something that was at the core of her being. She thrived in this office and her good relationship with comrades in higher positions enabled her to provide better service to her constituency. Mah had finally come full circle and was living her best life doing what she was born to do and she was loved by all.

Adorned with her sun hat, she would drive to inaccessible and godforsaken armpits of society. She sometimes had to leave her car and walk to reach homesteads that were concealed by their rural landscapes with a mission to change people's lives. A self-disciplined comrade, she reported for work in the civic centre offices very early in the morning and returned with the rest of the local workforce in the evenings. Her phone rang non-stop, and it never went unanswered. She answered and escalated cases of concern, attended meetings by street committees and Community Police Forums (CPF) and even intervened in community emergencies such as funding the funerals of destitute community members who faced the possibility of having pauper funerals.

Children who had not a shred of paper to confirm their identity were some of the cases she had to deal with every day. Following decades of political war, displaced orphans could not access free healthcare or government grants. She arranged to reunite them with their relatives so that they would no longer be wards of the state. Some experienced deliberate social exclusion due to their parents' political affiliations. Some orphans had children of their own, and some became that way because of the rampant HIV/ Aids pandemic. The issues and reasons for registration adversities could go on forever.

Health care was another point of crucial importance for her office. The establishment of home-based care volunteers was one of her most cherished ideas. She organised critical care and hospice admissions for the gravely ill and home caregivers for those who could recuperate at home.

That we would one day find ourselves without her was something we thought would never happen, maybe in her 80s and beyond because no one is immortal. They say that when you have run a good race, your name can be called anytime, and no one could deny that she had done and achieved more than most of her peers. She answered her call home at 62. That is too young for anyone to die.

Unbeknown to her, or anyone else, a silent killer known as cervical cancer had slowly crept up on her during her years at the Ward 96 office. Why has no one put an end to this raging python?

Cancer has become a rampant billion-dollar disease with no breakthroughs, even with all the millions poured into research by corporates, survivors, donors and governments. Doctor David Chan, an American oncologist and author of the book; Breast Cancer: Real Questions/Real Answers, echoes this. "I'll be the first to admit that despite all the billions put into cancer research, the expected result of preventing cancer and treating advanced cancer have been disappointing. Unlike reducing deaths from heart attacks and stroke, progress in reducing deaths from cancer has been disappointingly slow."

It continues to be an early detection and donation platform. Why does this disease continue to destroy people everywhere and with such brutality despite all the money and work involved?

People in the health sector say women in their menopause might ignore the signs because the milestone itself presents them with many odd new pains. First, they might think their period is making up for its disappearance of many months until they realise it cannot be. After a month or so of pain in their breasts or bleeding, they realise it's too much. Then they report the matter to the family. The same way my mom told my sister, who immediately took her to her gynaecologist. After running some tests, the doctor sadly confirmed that my mom had cervical cancer and started her on chemotherapy.

There is nothing therapeutic about chemotherapy. Every time she came back from the treatment, she was weaker and would sometimes throw up, finding it hard to keep anything in her stomach, which exacerbated her condition. Her hands darkened. She continued with the treatment and didn't lose a strand of hair, ironically. It was a good sign to us somehow. She seemed to be on the mend. The doctors said her cancer was in remission. But after one of her hospital check-ups, she was told the cervical cancer had spread to her lungs. What a harrowing experience! Then she had a stroke. It's a wonder we didn't suffer a stroke ourselves. Soon it spread to her brain. At this stage, she couldn't eat, see, or hear a thing.

Nozipho and I would just stare at her and back at each other in disbelief. It was shocking to come face to face with the ravages of this disease. At this stage, the doctors told us to take her and care for her at home. You know there's nothing more doctors can do for a patient when they ask you to take her home. We bought her a hospital bed and tried to spend as much time with her, but she just deteriorated to a point where we had to fly her to Umbumbulu, where she stayed only two days before succumbing to the disease. The date was August 07, 2008.

Upon hearing of her passing, Winnie Mandela called to request a postponement to the initial funeral date because the events of Women's Day placed demands on her time and she also wanted to attend her sister-in-the-struggle's funeral. In the struggle, people learnt of others' unwavering hard work and commitment and loved them from a distance because they worked hard in their different corners too. We honoured her wishes, and she graced the funeral with her presence. It was a huge state funeral service that had to be held at Sobhisi stadium with dignitaries from all over the country. Sbu Ndebele, Jeff Radebe, Zweli Mkhize, Obed Mlaba, Bheki Cele and others came out in their numbers. Gospel giants like Rebecca Malope, Deborah Frazer, Stimela and others gave her a fitting send-off. She was hailed as the lioness, a hero and a true comrade who was selfless and kept the flag flying through it all. She left behind three children, Nozipho, my younger brother S'phelele and myself together with 10 grandchildren. Four from S'bu, two from Nozipho, three from S'phelele and one from me. In the true nature of his Scorpio male profile, S'bu had led in all areas of his life and procreated from a tender age of 14 and didn't stop until he was 20. In fact, his last-born came into life on the day that he lost his. Could he have resurrected himself? I cannot imagine what that does to a new mother.

Three years before, on Human Rights Day, the eThekwini mayor Obed Mlaba named what was formerly known as the Martin West building on 251 Smith Street after mah. The Florence Mkhize building stands proudly next to the famous Royal hotel and eThekwini's largest library building.

S'BAHLE'S ACCIDENT

Sometimes, life has a way of showing us just how insignificant we are over the direction our lives take. Our lives are not in the palms of our hands. We may believe that we have wisdom, academic degrees and in fortunate circumstances, money but ultimately, all is in the hands of the creator. Ours is to stay the course, have faith and see the hand of the Lord.

I sometimes forget that I did not give birth to S'bahle, yet I consider her my first born through and through. I see so much of my strength in her because that is what I instilled in her. When I first met S'bahle, she was ten years old. I saw her as an answer to my prayers because of the initial negative stance I had on motherhood.

What a cute little thing with the most gorgeous eyes and smile! I immediately poured all my maternal love on her and felt an immediate connection with her. I remember that I just wanted to love and protect her from the beginning. I was also so thankful that her mother didn't give us problems with raising her. Some parents struggle to allow others to raise their children no matter the circumstances. Especially black people. There is still a lot of stigma associated with adoption. People warn, "What if the child has an incurable disease, what if they turn out to be a criminal later in life? What if this happens? What if that happens?"

This is when I recall one of the most significant quotes about children and parenting by author and painter Khalil Gibran:

"Your children are not your children.
They are the sons and daughters of Life's longing for itself.
They come through you but not from you.
And though they are with you yet they belong not to you.
You may give them your love but not your thoughts,
For they have their own thoughts.
You may house their bodies but not their souls,
For their souls dwell in the house of tomorrow, which you cannot visit, not even in your dreams.
You may strive to be like them but seek not to make them like you.
For life goes not backward nor tarries with yesterday.

You are the bows from which your children as living arrows are sent forth.
The archer sees the mark upon the path of the infinite, and He bends you
with His might that His arrows may go swift and far.
Let your bending in the archer's hand be for gladness.
For even as He loves the arrow that flies, so He loves also the bow that is
stable."

Very few ask positive questions. Perhaps it's because of the trauma in black society. They encourage people to adopt within the family lineage. I guess that helped my course when I decided to raise S'bahle. She was my husband's child and by extension, my child.

We developed an open and democratic relationship as she got older. I had "The Big Talk" with her when she reached puberty. I want to believe I was the first person she talked to about dating her first boyfriend when she came of age. We do not own our children, so I didn't object. I just had to escalate the talk and make it more relevant to the reality at hand. Raising a girl is not easy. As a mother, before a girl is mature enough, you sort of censor yourself even when you advise about sex education, neatness and cleanliness. You wonder, is this information too much too soon? Am I overly domesticating her? Might it lead her astray or turn her completely against relationships? Could she develop a negative opinion about house chores? Big ups to people who have multiple children of both sexes.

As S'bahle came into her own after graduating with a bachelor's degree in Housing and Town Planning from the University of KwaZulu-Natal, I realised I may have exceeded the independent thinking dosage. She decided she wanted to be a personal trainer despite her initial wish to become a big shot in the construction sector. I thought she would join the family business, but as in the true soapie storyline, she decided to off-ramp and do her own thing. Was I upset with this decision? Let us say not as much as I would have been if she had chosen our wishes over hers. I was glad that she saw it through to graduation. A different child would have jumped ship without thinking twice. Our children rightfully have more options.

I was very proud to see her doing her own thing and doing it so well. After taking me through this new social media influencer community, and how she could make money from it, I was sold. Her brand was growing rapidly with a following of over a million. She got busy and pushed it too. She had marketing campaigns, local and far. Some went as far as Botswana and she started modelling gym and underwear brands, I was gobsmacked. Next, she was on magazine covers and travelling around the world. What had I done?

She also participated in season eight of the Tropika Island Treasure. A popular television soap opera, Muvhango auditioned her for a role. She was awaiting a call back when my phone rang that fateful morning of Thursday, August 09, 2018. I had spent the night at my sister, Nozipho's place. So confused and dazed was I that I initially rushed to the accident scene before I remembered that paramedics had rushed her to hospital after finding her entrapped in her car on Victoria Embankment in Durban. Upon arrival at the hospital, I discovered that she was critically injured and was fighting for her life in ICU.

It was one of the most awful calls of my entire life. The only information I received at first was that she had been driving on Margaret Mncadi Avenue and that emergency officials had to use the Jaws of Life to remove her from her overturned vehicle. They also said there was no other car involved. I later learnt she had broken all the bones in her body, both arms, both legs and toes. Her face was another medley of broken bones, hanging eye sockets, broken jaws and a cracked mouth. Even her fingers were broken. How was she still alive I wondered in gratitude!

I arrived at the hospital where doctors wanted exorbitant fees upfront before they could even touch her. Unfortunately, she cancelled her medical aid a month before. The worst was when I had to consent to have her induced into a medical coma. I was afraid of the risk, yet I was more terrified of the pain she would be in if she remained conscious. The medical team advised me of the ramifications of my decision and implications, which included blood clots, pneumonia, heart problems, vivid nightmares and hallucinations. At this point, anything that did not have death as a side effect was okay with me. Could she just live? At only 23, she had so much to live for!

And so started S'bahle's journey to recovery. We relied strictly on doctors' reports. A lot of medical jargon in drips and drabs accompanied the little information that we received. The medical fraternity is the least comforting in times of distress. Their language was not very compassionate. They kept to the facts at a time when comfort and positivity were what we needed. Meanwhile, her stay in hospital was a combination of surgical procedures and family fears. We wondered if she would pull through to walk on her own, retain her sight and enjoy the practicalities necessary for a quality life. Little things like knowing her healthy lifestyle before the accident would contribute to her healing comforted us. Doctors also attributed her rapid recovery to this.

We were still worried about the disfigurement of her face. She had scars all over. How would it affect her self-esteem and career? It was a long time for the anxious. Days became weeks, weeks became months, and then a miracle happened.

When she finally came around, we were so happy for the air in her lungs. We also learnt that her spinal cord was left intact. What a relief! These are the little things that help families of accident survivors cope. First, you go through the shock, the trauma, the hope and then gratitude for the mercies we usually take for granted about the gift of life.

Having been warned about amnesia, I was not too worried when she stared blankly. Then she started by talking as if she was in her high school class. She asked me during one of the visits to ring her high school principal and tell her she was still stuck in the hospital. According to her, she had fallen from the stairs in school. I was hopeful that it was temporary. Otherwise, how would we begin reconstructing so many memories? This was better than the initial dots of her life where she was like a blank sheet. It was heart breaking. It was a confounding situation yet we remained hopeful. I guess we all worried that she might even lose her sense of identity in the aftermath. For some people, amnesia can be permanent.

Some people would sob at this discovery, but my responsibility was to do everything to make sure her memory was stimulated. The medical procedure for memory restoration alone cost R15 000 a month. I would also always ensure to ask questions that would trigger her memory. I brought out family albums and took her to her favourite spots when she was fit enough. You cannot imagine my happiness when she started slowly to show signs of remembering. She called me one day and told me she dreamt up my number and was just calling to find out whom the owner of the number was. I had to reintroduce myself to her and we laughed it off. Our biggest hope was that eventually, she could remember what happened minutes before the accident, so we would have an idea even if it would not undo the accident. According to her, the accident happened in a split second. She approached a curve at normal speed but hit the curved road's guardrails, which caused her to hit her head against her door which caused her to pass out.

At that moment, she had more stressful things to worry about. Like the fact that she now had to use a wheelchair to get around and be mindful of that awful leg brace around her leg. It looked dangerous and sore but as a mother, you must put on a brave face and act as if such things are small fry otherwise your child takes her cues from you. If you break down, she breaks down too. It is a difficult thing to do but these are some of the bitter fruits of motherhood. The trauma rendered her powerless.

She was terrified of hurting herself and I was worried sick she would get too comfortable in her wheelchair. I had to be strict about her physical movement. I did not mince my words about her putting her mind to it. I would wear my severe face and rebuke her contentment in the wheelchair because I feared muscle retardation. So, I got her a personal trainer as soon as she was able to move her limbs.

I am a person of milestones. They started with the upper body, and I was happy with that, but I would be lying if I said I didn't 'want them to get to the legs already. Our great concern was her lower body, where her mobility had to resume. Having been raised by a medical mother, I encouraged the mind over matter principle. In the same way, I encouraged her to tackle the world with the vigour it demanded. I hope I was also patient enough to realise we were dealing with a patient now, not the fitness bunny we had known all our lives. One foot in front of the other was my mission with her healing process. One day at a time!

You cannot imagine the victory and glee I felt when one day, without any warning, S'bahle came to my office and got off the wheelchair to take a few steps. I suspect she had been practising to give me a show because she was not a girl who had just discovered she could walk again. Those were too many steps for a first attempt. She managed to do so because the brace had been removed and she only wore a moon boot. I was beyond thrilled! This act ushered so much hope. At last, she could remember motion and things could only get better. A clearer memory would follow her ability to move independently. She started remembering people, places and events although she did call me again at another time to ask who I was. I had to remind her again that she had called me on my other number.

The sad thing about amnesia is that even though people might recall incidents and faces, they sometimes lose the emotions attached to people. My daughter forgot her feelings for her fiancé Itumeleng Khune. Wait, what? You don't remember the man with whom you thought you would share the rest of your life? It must have been devastating for him. She said she didn't remember why she had fallen in love with him and who can blame her? This young woman had come out of a dark place. Not that I could ever claim to relate but she had come out of it - scars and all!

MY WANDERLUST

When former president Thabo Mbeki first recited the poem, I Am an African, at the passing of the new Constitution of South Africa on 8 May 1996, it stirred an array of emotions in me. It was a momentous event because he was declaring the legitimacy of the work of my mom and her comrades. It is rather a long poem but here it is:

"I am an African.

I owe my being to the hills and the valleys, the mountains and the glades, the rivers, the deserts, the trees, the flowers, the seas, and the ever-changing seasons that define the face of our native land.

My body has frozen in our frosts and in our latter-day snows. It has thawed in the warmth of our sunshine and melted in the heat of the midday sun. The crack and the rumble of the summer thunders, lashed by startling lightening, have been a cause both of trembling and of hope.

The fragrances of nature have been as pleasant to us as the sight of the wild blooms of the citizens of the veld.

The dramatic shapes of the Drakensberg, the soil-coloured waters of the Lekoa, iGqili noThukela, and the sands of the Kgalagadi, have all been panels of the set on the natural stage on which we act out the foolish deeds of the theatre of our day.

At times, and in fear, I have wondered whether I should concede equal citizenship of our country to the leopard and the lion, the elephant and the springbok, the hyena, the black mamba and the pestilential mosquito.

A human presence among all these, a feature on the face of our native land thus defined, I know that none dare challenge me when I say - I am an African!

I owe my being to the Khoi and the San whose desolate souls haunt the great expanses of the beautiful Cape - they who fell victim to the most merciless genocide our native land has ever seen, they who were the first to lose their lives in the struggle to defend our freedom and dependence and they who, as a people, perished in the result..."

I know it sounds cliché to reiterate, but we truly live in a beautiful country. A country where the landscape, the seasons, the crops and the people are awesome. Have you ever seen the torrents of rain and the rainbow that unleashes its glory soon after? Sometimes we get two rainbows in one village. As expansive as South Africa is, there isn't a province without its show of splendour. KZN for instance could be three or four countries in one province with its sparkling oceans, rolling hills and greenery. No wonder the Big Five and their cousins have continued to thrive decades after the prophesy of doom. We could do better in nature conservation but all in all, we are a beautiful country. Our economy is in a dire state but that is a matter of politics.

I have been to countries where the landscape is impressive, but the food is dull. Sometimes you are in a country where sports is a way of life but the heinous crimes defy this beauty. We have our alarming crime rates that even inspire foreigners to commit crimes on our shores. People such as Anni Dewani, whose husband arranged her murder after she studied and analysed crime in our country. The FBI also pounced on what they called the romance scammers in our beautiful city of Cape Town. However, I must have faith that this is not the future of our country.

Others boast thriving economies but have no humanity. Two stories about Oprah Winfrey's shopping excursions remind me of this fact. In the first story, she says she was in Roma, Italy and wanted to buy a Louis Vuitton handbag for her friend's teenage daughter after she had pointed at the bag through the window. They went in to purchase the item, only for the sales assistant to refuse vehemently to sell them the bag. He started by saying the handbag was made exclusively for Italians. "Perhaps if you go back to your own country, you can get a bag..." she regaled her audience. The Oprah Winfrey Show didn't air in Italy, so that could be one of the reasons that the assistant failed to recognise Oprah. After making light of the situation, a local tour guide was called in and after he spoke to the assistant, it was agreed she could buy the handbag. However, the young woman had changed her mind by then and wanted another bag, which was blasphemous in the eyes of the sales assistant. Eventually and perhaps after he was made to understand who Oprah was, the agreement was followed by a festive mood, where champagne appeared out of nowhere. End of that story.

When a similar incident happened in Switzerland, the tourism department sent a formal public apology. The media covered the story, which changed the tone of that experience, especially when she later said the apology was not necessary. Unlike Italy, they performed reputational damage control for their country's dignity.

This also reminds me of my travels through France. Since I was young, I had an undying wish to see, smell, touch and experience Paris. The marketing around the country has been unwavering. Renowned for its fashion houses, classical monuments like the Eiffel Tower and sophisticated cuisine, it's every romantic's dream destination. But beware of the hostility if you do not speak the language. The French will speak their language to you whether you understand it or not. I find that very distasteful. Don't get me wrong. There is no disputing that the language is beautiful. So beautiful in fact, it is said that English has about 30 per cent of its words like chic, déjà vu and veneer borrowed from the language. But unless you can say, "Bonjour, Merci, Je m'appelle Shauwn..." and proceed into a full-blown conversation, forget it - you won't make much progress. They get ten out of ten for a rich history, sophistication and thriving tourism of 9.7 per cent GDP, which supports 2.9 million jobs. However, you had better register for a French degree if you want to enjoy your stay in that country.

In Brazil, I marvelled at the picturesque beaches and deft hospitality service. You sit there and it feels so surreal it is as if you are sitting on a travel page of Vogue magazine. The young women in that part of the world will show you a thing or two about beauty. Because of the stark differences between the haves and the have-nots, most women invest in their beauty and bodies to level the playing field. Most are said to be in debt as there are beauty clinics that provide Botox, body sculpting, veneers, hair implants, and the works, on credit.

To further bridge the gap, low-income earners build their favelas right across lavish five-star hotels and other important national spots. A favela is a shantytown. The difference with favelas is they are as old as history itself dating back to the 19th century. They have harboured sports excellence, poverty and crime. A New York Times article spoke of a man who had 23 siblings from a woman who prostituted herself to feed them. He spoke of how he had to share an egg with six other people. In the end, he sold his kidney for $6,000 to a middleman involved in organ trading. He is not the only one; many Brazilians sell organs like eye corneas, liver, kidneys and lungs. In 2018, the World Health Organisation (WHO) estimated that as many as 10 000 organs were trafficked every year.

For most countries, the problem is the weather or banality, sometimes both. For cities like New York, that is not a bother. The weather can be icy with temperatures threatening hypothermia, yet I have not seen a more enticing city for shopping. There are beautiful clothing shops everywhere. Everywhere! Restaurants offer servings enough for three people. Food is also very affordable in the USA. We spend 14 per cent more on food compared to the Americans. Their low cost of food production can be attributed to the government's investment in agricultural technology. As a result, obesity is a problem.

The place I fell in love with and keep yearning for is Monaco, for obvious reasons. To give you an idea of how royal the country is; their prisoners have chefs cooking them three-course meals. Thirty-two per cent of the country's population are millionaires. The poverty rate is zero. All these people are guaranteed one police officer per hundred of them. Who would not have a life expectancy of 84 years with such a soft life?

What I would love to see more of are our African countries. I have been to a few and would love to see all 53. I have seen more countries outside of Africa. I understand why wealthy families allow their children to take a gap year to travel. Nothing will teach you invaluable life lessons more than travel. It opens your eyes, humbles you, shakes you into reality, hooks you with its awe, moulds you and elevates your sense of wonder. You cannot travel and remain the same. It is impossible.

WOMEN OF POWER

I have my own role models. People I have looked up to whether consciously or subconsciously as I was coming into my own. Their leadership traits have shaped my own decision-making and leadership skills. For instance, there is a bit of mah in me, naturally. Her humanitarian work has affected how I look at less advantaged people. I have had to appoint people to manage my philanthropy because I have been inundated with financial requests. In instances where it has been possible, I have been able to assist immediately. Where requests were the same, I have had to apply myself. One of the lessons I learnt from my mom about philanthropy is that you disempower people from living their lives by giving them too much.

This is where the concept of the caterpillar comes in again. Your generosity cannot be to the extent that you leave your beneficiary needing more help in the future. I believe in the ability of all human beings to conquer adversity and that this ability is honed by time. In adversity lies the possibility of a breakthrough.

Mum also taught us to live a life of purpose. Being a layabout was always vehemently opposed at home. The first step towards this life of determination is to wake up early. I am usually up as early as 5 am and sometimes earlier to prepare for the day ahead. I run several businesses and if I left things to chance, some businesses might never get my undivided attention.

Obviously, Oprah is one of my role models. Her worldly intelligence and genuine personality have instilled wonder in me. The fact that such an important person owns up to her flaws, current and ancient makes her a woman of good standing to me. In one of her interviews, she spoke about how she initially modelled her career around media personality Barbara Walters and spent too much time moulding her questions to sound clever rather than listen attentively. I think that is just remarkable. You can only learn from your own mistakes, and she is living proof of that.

Even her flip side; bruised from sexual abuse, insecurity and a weight loss journey has been the topic of discussion in many a dining room. Her legacy has been entrenched in truth. It's never easy but Oprah makes it look that way, especially as she is also blessed with eloquence. The two paramount lessons I have learnt from her are, 1. You have the right to say no. 2. You have the right to change your mind. That is leadership!

As a business leader who mentors others, I must learn from giants such as the women mentioned above. Not because I want to be exactly like them, but because we all have different contributions to make to society. We also must evolve to play our roles more effectively. It is important to learn and incorporate from role models and mentors.

I am also inspired by; surprise – surprise - Beyoncé. The girl is magic on two legs. Her concerts are dazzling; she captures the audience, inspires others to do better and balances the gender scale. When she does her thing on stage or in videos, you can see the extent of blood and sweat during rehearsals. She is an icon. Yet she works as if she is still trying to make a name for herself. If that is not an example of the determination of a giant, gallantry, and all things colossal - I do not know what is. Here is someone whose brand has been consistent for a solid 19 years, looks 25 even though she is 40 and yet still managed to draw 2.24 million fans during The Formation World Tour in 2016. Michael Jackson managed a whopping 4 million fan attendance during his Dangerous Tour in 1992. But then there were not as many people with television sets and social media did not exist back then.

Finally, our beloved Winnie Madikizela-Mandela. How is it that she was sophistication personified and a no-nonsense taker at the same time? She was pretty, well spoken, fearless and liberated. There are photos taken during the Rivonia Trial that personify her personal style.

Admittedly, Mam'Winnie was no angel, but it is public knowledge how much she sacrificed her own and her children's lives for the liberation of the people. Like my mom and I, her parents also expected a boy when she was in her mom's womb and bam - there she was. She was vilified as a vigilante who ordered killings and after the findings by the TRC, she never admitted to the accusations against her. Then Nelson Mandela divorced her and she did not even become a minister. Yet she carried herself with great dignity looking fabulous in all political and social events. She was leadership personified, through and through!

To my hero...

DEAR S'BU

The sun went down the day you died. Not just for me. For Mom, Nozipho and S'phelele. The entire province mourned your death. You were the brother I wish other girls my age had. The one who was so gifted, so outgoing with so much to live for, you were the sunshine of our home. I could never tell my story without mentioning you. How your bravery, juvenile as it was, changed the course of our lives forever. Philosophers talk about the role of prodigals in every developing society. Nevertheless, you assumed the role of a father at such a young age; I guess you were the chosen one for us. If only for a little while.

It hurts so much that your children did not get to know you. Your tenacity and your sharp dance moves that we cannot even imitate because they were so deft. Do you have any idea of the difficulty of describing to a child, the kind of person their father was, especially when he died young? I can only imagine what goes through their minds as they try to process why fate left them without a father. To us who were left without a beloved brother, it cuts deeper. Sometimes it's better to have not known so much greatness. But then again, the world would have been poorer without you. It is broke without you. I know you would have been a great leader. You also would make a great dad. As great as our father.

Did he cross examine you when you got to the other side? Was he livid or understanding? I hope for the latter. Happy memories collide with sadness as I realise that we never know the hour. We had given up on your life long before you were so gruesomely taken from us. Had I known your trip back to Transkei would be the last, I would have given you the longest embrace.

I wonder sometimes, was the short life you lived as full as it should have been? You were too young - gone too soon. Did you get a hero's welcome where you are? Did you see Bridgeman and Msizi? Were you watching as your son was born on the day you died?

When the funeral arrangements were underway, I realized you would never get to see me graduate, get married, have children, or drive my first car. You would have loved our children S'bu.

I have acquired much in my life and I live comfortably. But if I were to choose between my accomplishments and having you alive, I wouldn't think twice about it. None of the earthly possessions can replace you in our hearts even though a part of me realises you have been our angel of abundant blessings. May you forever hold this lamp of light above us all. Especially for your beautiful children.

Always on our minds, forever in our hearts!

PS I have not deviated from your teachings. I do not trust too much anymore. They also don't make the Jazz cologne anymore.

Printed in the United States
by Baker & Taylor Publisher Services